AF809432

HEALING BLACK FATIGUE

Practices for Renewal, Joy, and Reclaiming Our Humanity

MARY-FRANCES WINTERS
MAREISHA N. WINTERS REESE

Berrett-Koehler
PUBLISHERS

Copyright © 2026 by Mary-Frances Winters and Mareisha N. Winters Reese

All rights reserved. No portion of this work may be reproduced or transmitted in any form or by any means, electronic or mechanical, including photocopying and recording, or by any information storage or retrieval system, or be used in training generative artificial intelligence (AI) technologies or developing machine-learning language models without permission, except in the case of brief quotations embodied in critical reviews and certain other noncommercial uses permitted by copyright law. For permission requests, please contact the Copyright Clearance Center at marketplace.copyright.com/rs-ui-web/mp.

Berrett-Koehler Publishers, Inc.
1333 Broadway, Suite P100
Oakland, CA 94612-1921
(510) 817-2277
bkconnection.com

Ordering Information
Quantity sales. Special discounts are available on quantity purchases by corporations, associations, individuals, and others. For details, please go to bkconnection.com to see our bulk discounts or contact bookorders@bkpub.com for more information.
Textbook exam/desk copies. Please consult the General FAQ at bkconnection.com.
Bookstore orders for trade or textbook use. For print books, please contact Penguin Random House Publisher Services at customerservice@penguinrandomhouse.com. For ebooks, contact your favorite distributor.

Distributed to the US trade and internationally by Penguin Random House Publisher Services.

The authorized representative in the EU for product safety and compliance is EU Compliance Partner, Pärnu mnt. 139b-14, 11317 Tallinn, Estonia, www.eucompliancepartner.com, +372 5368 65 02.

Berrett-Koehler and the BK logo are registered trademarks of Berrett-Koehler Publishers, Inc.

Printed in the United States of America

Berrett-Koehler books are printed on long-lasting acid-free paper. When it is available, we choose paper that has been manufactured by environmentally responsible processes. These may include using trees grown in sustainable forests, incorporating recycled paper, minimizing chlorine in bleaching, or recycling the energy produced at the paper mill.

Cataloging-in-Publication Data is on file at the Library of Congress
Library of Congress Control Number: 2026019748
9798890572592 paperback | 9798890572608 pdf | 9798890572615 epub

First Edition
35 34 33 32 31 30 29 28 27 26 10 9 8 7 6 5 4 3 2 1

Book production: Happenstance Type-O-Rama
Cover design: Ashley Ingram with Mike Nichols

Dear Black People . . .

May we be met with softness where the
world has been hard.

May our bodies experience rest without guilt and joy
that needs no explanation.

May we release what was never ours to carry—
urgency, over-functioning, constant proving—
and welcome ease without apology.

May our healing be deep and on our own terms.

May our laughter be loud and unpoliced.

May our boundaries be honored, especially by ourselves.

May we be supported, protected, and surrounded
by a community that sees us, love that sustains us, and
ancestors who continue to whisper: You are not alone.

May we dream boldly and live gently.

May we choose ourselves again and again.

And may we live in a world where Black life is not
just survived, but nourished, celebrated, and free.

CONTENTS

PREFACE

Healing Black Fatigue was written in response to the question that arose after the publication of the first edition of our book, *Black Fatigue: How Racism Erodes the Mind, Body, and Spirit*. Now that we have language for naming Black fatigue, how do we heal?

This book attempts to provide some answers to that question: *Black Fatigue* articulated the condition, and *Healing Black Fatigue* explores pathways toward restoration, wholeness, and sustained well-being.

Healing Black Fatigue is also a response to the historical moment in which it was written. During the Trump era—both terms, but especially the second—we have witnessed an alarming normalization of political polarization, dehumanization, and legislated racism. Immigration practices that separate families, detention centers that ignore human suffering, the erosion of civil and human rights protections, and an increasing resistance to honest (or any) conversations about race, inequity, and the history that shaped our current circumstances. The impact has been devastating, especially for marginalized communities.

For those of us who have devoted our professional lives to diversity, equity, inclusion, justice, and crosscultural understanding, this environment has been excruciatingly fatiguing. Mary-Frances has spent more than four decades in the field of diversity, equity, and inclusion (DEI) in service of bringing people of different backgrounds together for greater understanding, respect, and cultural competence. Mareisha has continued that work for more than fourteen years at The Winters Group. To witness a palpable retreat from these values, fueled by fear, intimidation, misinformation, disinformation, racism, and moral cowardice, has taken its toll.

We name this context not to center ourselves or our work, but to be honest about its impact. The backlash against DEI has not reduced the need for justice-centered efforts; it has intensified it. At the same time, it has exacerbated Black fatigue, deepening the weariness carried by those most affected by injustice and those committed to addressing it.

Healing Black Fatigue is intended to be both a response and a refusal: a response to accelerating harm, and a refusal to capitulate to lies and more dehumanization. Even in these troubling times, healing remains possible, and this book is designed to support you on that journey.

This book is written first and foremost for people of African descent—across the diaspora, in the Motherland, across generations, and across lived experiences. It is for those carrying visible and invisible fatigue from systems that, for centuries, have not acknowledged our full humanity. It is for those who are weary of having to prove, explain, adapt, or endure in environments that repeatedly demand resilience without offering restoration.

At the same time, the book is intentionally inclusive. It is also written for other marginalized and historically oppressed groups whose lives have been shaped by colonization, enslavement, displacement, and systemic inequity—while history differs, the consequences of exclusion, erasure, and chronic stress are often shared. And it is written for allies, practitioners, and professionals, including educators, social workers, healthcare providers, therapists, DEI practitioners, organizational leaders, and others who recognize that policies and strategies alone cannot heal the kind of fatigue that comes from historical trauma and is embodied.

This is not a manual, a checklist, or a promise that healing is quick, linear, or simple. This book does not ask readers to be more resilient or to adapt endlessly to systems that remain unchanged. Instead, it offers reflections, frameworks, and practices grounded in African-centered psychology, ancestral wisdom, communal traditions, and contemporary research.

At its core, *Healing Black Fatigue* is about remembering who we are beyond the characterizations of those who know nothing about us. It is about restoring balance where imbalance has been normalized, reclaiming joy without justification, and reconnecting to sources of wisdom and strength that predate the harm.

We share some of our own healing stories and those of others in our various circles. They are stories of joy and pain, progress and roadblocks, hope and despair. But through it all, still we rise, and it is our hope that after reading *Healing Black Fatigue*, you too will rise.

May this book meet you where you are and walk with you as you continue forward.

It is our honor to share our insights with you.

MUCH LOVE,
Mary-Frances and Mareisha

INTRODUCTION

FROM FATIGUE TO FLOURISHING

Note on capitalization: We capitalize "Black" and lowercase "white" when referring to these two identity groups, following Brookings's 2020 decision, after months of research, to update its style guide in this way. Brookings's rationale is as follows: "It is an act in recognition of racial respect for those who have been generations in the 'lower case.'"[1]

Healing Black Fatigue: Practices for Renewal, Joy, and Reclaiming Our Humanity expands the conversation from our book *Black Fatigue: How Racism Erodes the Mind, Body, and Spirit*, from understanding the detrimental impacts of Black fatigue to exploring how Black people and communities can live, remain whole, and even flourish amid persistent racialized stress.

Black fatigue gives language to an intergenerational phenomenon many Black people have long carried but perhaps could not name. It articulates what countless individuals feel in their bodies and spirits, yet have been conditioned and even forced to normalize. Black fatigue is the cumulative toll of racism, bias, exclusion, vigilance, and the constant need to navigate systems that were never designed with Black humanity in mind. In *Black Fatigue*, we define it as the repeated variations of stress that result in extreme exhaustion and cause mental, physical, and spiritual maladies that are passed down from generation to generation.

When the first edition of *Black Fatigue* was published in 2020, the world was in the midst of an intense racial reckoning. The COVID-19 pandemic put a spotlight on the stark preexisting racial disparities in health outcomes, economic insecurity, and disproportionate access to care. The murders of George Floyd, Breonna Taylor, Ahmaud Arbery, and others around the same time ignited global protests and renewed conversations about race, justice, and accountability. Organizations, institutions, and governments issued statements, launched initiatives, and pledged commitments to diversity, equity, and inclusion, with a specific focus on antiracism. For a brief moment, it appeared hopeful that the depth and persistence of racial harm were finally being acknowledged. However, that hope was fleeting.

The second edition, published in June 2026, highlights the 180-degree turn in government and, to an extent, corporate policies that took place between 2020 and 2025. It also provides an updated look at the conditions and inequities examined in the first edition, revealing that rather than abating, most persist or have even worsened.

Many of the same forces that have historically fueled Black fatigue have reemerged even more brazenly in the second Trump administration. We have witnessed the dismantling of human rights protections, the rollback of DEI initiatives, and even the prohibition of conversations about race and racism. There has been an overt relegitimization of policies, practices, rhetoric, and untruths that minimize, dismiss, and weaponize the realities of racism. Across the United States and around the globe, the emotional whiplash has been profound, exacerbating Black fatigue as the burden to fight this deleterious trend falls, as usual, mostly on Black people. What can we do about it? While there are no easy answers, this book offers strategies that support restoration, renewal, and the ability to sustain wholeness amid accelerating anti-Black racism.

Calling on the Ancestors

Black fatigue is not a fleeting condition. It is not simply burnout, nor is it stress that can be resolved through better habits or individual resilience alone. Black fatigue is systemic, cumulative, and intergenerational. It lives in the nervous system, in cultural memory, in families, workplaces, schools, and institutions. It is reinforced and compounded by repeated exposure to inequity, ~~micro~~aggressions, and overt discrimination, and the psychological labor required to navigate racialized environments while maintaining dignity, self-worth, and physical and mental well-being. (Note: As in *Black Fatigue*, we intentionally cross out "micro" because the impacts of these aggressions are anything but small.)

At the same time, Black cultures have always possessed the knowledge and the practices to survive, resist, heal, and flourish. Long before modern language around trauma, mental health, or well-being entered mainstream discourse, African and Indigenous traditions emphasized balance, spirituality, community, ritual, rest, movement, storytelling, and joy as essential to human life. These practices were not supplemental, they were foundational for survival.

Healing Black Fatigue draws on some of those deep traditions while engaging contemporary scholarship in trauma-informed psychology, neuroscience, public health, leadership, and organizational behavior. It does not suggest that individuals can think, reflect, or meditate their way out of systemic racism. Structural change, accountability, and collective action remain essential. But personal, communal, and ancestral practices are also essential. Without healing, fatigue morphs into depletion, and depletion becomes despair. And despair is precisely what unjust systems depend on to sustain themselves.

A Conversation Across Generations

This book is also deeply personal and written in the voices of two generations.

Mary-Frances

I have been leading The Winters Group for more than four decades—forty-two years as of March 2026—navigating corporate, institutional, and global systems that were rarely designed with Black humanity, let alone Black women's leadership, in mind. Throughout those decades, I have seen cycles of progress and retrenchment. I have witnessed moments when the language of inclusion gained traction, only to be stripped of its meaning or abandoned without real change being actualized. I discovered that working, living, and leading in racialized spaces demanded more than competence; it demanded endurance, vigilance, and a sustained commitment to grounding myself in purpose and values.

I came of age at a time when survival itself felt like success. There were no road maps and few role models for Black women—no language for the exhaustion that settled, unnamed, into the body after years of being the only one, the first one, or the exception. You learned to carry it. Fatigue was rarely named; it was simply normalized.

I learned how racism rears its ugly head in so many different ways. It shows up in lowered expectations and heightened scrutiny, in being objectified, in being sought out for wisdom but excluded from power, in being invited to the table yet expected to sit in silence. I endured corporate America for a decade before, out of sheer frustration, I started my own business in 1984. It was such a novelty that the local newspaper featured me in an article titled "Woman Starts Business in Her Basement." Little did I know that I was pioneering in more ways than one; starting a small business, let alone one from home, was still a rarity.

These years as an entrepreneur have not been easy, but I do not regret forging my own way rather than staying in what I experienced as a repressive, fatiguing environment that refused to see my full humanity. Running my own business by no means shields me from the inequities I speak about here, but the difference is that I have had more power to make decisions in service of my well-being. What has sustained me is not simply endurance, but grounding—an internal compass shaped by elders, ancestors, friends, family, faith, and an understanding that my worth is not determined by a power structure that either consciously or unconsciously sees me as less than. I came to understand I was never carrying these burdens alone. Surrounded by a large and supportive network of family, friends, and colleagues, many of whom share identical or similar experiences with anti-Black racism, I have been able to navigate Black fatigue.

In this book, Mareisha and I will share some strategies—our own and others'—for dealing with Black fatigue. What we hope readers will gain is the understanding that healing is about choosing more than survival. It is about restoring balance where imbalance has been normalized, about reclaiming joy without apology, about leading authentically despite what Toni Morrison calls being under the scrutiny of the "white gaze," where whiteness functions as the default norm through which Black people are seen, judged, and valued. As one of many examples of the white gaze in my corporate experience, during a period when I was wearing a short afro hairstyle, one of my colleagues suggested that if I wanted to succeed, I should straighten my hair and let it grow. At the time, I was in my mid-twenties, and I reluctantly conformed. Hopefully, this book will help provide the generations that have come after me and those that will come after them with the courage and strategies to resist.

Mareisha

I entered the workforce at the beginning of the 21st century with different tools than my mother, but I encountered familiar challenges. My degrees—BSs in electrical engineering and computer science, an MBA, and an MS in information systems—were supposed to guarantee me a seat at the table. Instead, my credentials were often met with doubt or surprise. In white, male-dominated science, technology, engineering, and math (STEM) environments, I learned quickly that expertise did not guarantee belonging, and technical competence did not shield me from bias. I found myself having to prove myself repeatedly and code-switch constantly.

In the corporate world, fatigue manifested for me as constant vigilance—living in environments where every move had to be calculated. My quiet, introverted nature was often interpreted as a lack of confidence or ambition, reinforcing the awareness that my competence could be discounted and my presence misinterpreted. That strain made going to work every day a struggle. A generation later, racism still lived in systems and processes that mirrored the same inequities my mother had faced, only now dressed in the alluring language of inclusion and belonging.

And yet, I also inherited something powerful: legacy. I did not enter these spaces without lineage. I relied on my mother's and others in her generation's experiences for support, guidance, and wisdom. Our professional paths unfolded in different eras and industries, yet the underlying dynamics were very similar.

That intergenerational wisdom, which we highlight throughout the book, taught me that I did not have to stay in such environments. After almost the same amount of time my mother spent in white-dominated spaces, I joined The Winters Group, and it was the best decision I could have made. As my mother mentioned, running a small business is not easy, but I feel liberated—able to be my authentic self in an environment where I am valued and respected not only for my expertise, but simply for being me.

And I want readers to know that there is a path for you as well. It may not be my path, but when we realize that the fatigue, learned helplessness, or imposter syndrome we feel is not a personal failing but a manifestation of deeply entrenched racist systems, endless possibilities open up: We can turn deficit thinking into asset thinking and live joyous, fulfilling lives that do not demand exhaustion as the price of participation.

Together

Our collective experiences affirm an undeniable truth: Black fatigue does not end with time, education, credentials, or professional success. In many cases, those achievements increase exposure to racialized stress. And yet, our stories also reflect continuity of resilience, wisdom, and hope. It is not about passing the baton to the next generation, but rather sharing it to make our impact even stronger. And that is what we attempt to do in this book. It is not a set of instructions but insights, reflections, and strategies we have found useful for navigating Black fatigue. It asks what becomes possible when we illuminate the spirit, honor the body, and remember ourselves as a community. If Black fatigue is the erosion, healing is the act of restoration—intentional, collective, and rooted in dignity.

Not a Destination or Prescription

Healing Black Fatigue is organized into four interconnected parts that reflect a holistic, ongoing healing journey rather than a linear progression with a fixed beginning and end. Instead of offering prescriptive solutions or rigid formulas, the book invites readers into a reflective exploration of how to navigate a racialized world while maintaining dignity, humanity, joy, and pride. It emphasizes self-awareness, agency, and communal support as essential responses to systemic racism. The guidance is designed to be adaptable for individuals, families, classrooms, community spaces, and faith communities, as well as workplaces.

While this book includes reflective prompts and suggested actions, it is not a workbook. There are no assignments to complete or outcomes to measure. Instead, the prompts and activities serve as invitations to pause, to reflect, to reconnect, and to choose practices that restore rather than deplete. It honors that there are multiple ways of knowing and recognizes that healing is a process.

Part I, Reclaiming Your Identity, explores how Black fatigue manifests in the body, mind, and spirit. It invites readers to name what they are carrying, examine internalized narratives, and locate themselves honestly within larger systems. Some of the concepts draw from African-centered psychology and Indigenous wisdom, traditions that understand personal well-being as inseparable from culture, spirituality, community, and history and that embrace the notion of the extended self. Unlike Western psychological models that often individualize trauma and pathologize responses to oppression, African-centered psychology and Indigenous wisdom recognize that much of what we experience as fatigue is a rational response to prolonged structural harm.

Part II, Reclaiming Power, Agency, and Voice, focuses on restoring choice, boundaries, resistance, purpose, and self-definition. Continuing to draw on African-centered psychology's emphasis on the extended self, this section affirms that agency is both personal and collective.

Part III, Healing Practices for Daily Renewal, offers grounding practices rooted in African ancestral and Indigenous wisdom, somatic awareness, spirituality, and contemporary research. These practices acknowledge that healing must be sustainable and accessible within the realities of everyday life. Central to this worldview is the Kemetic concept of *Sakhu Djaer*, often described as "the illumination of the spirit." *Sakhu* refers to the process of remembering who we are at our core—beyond imposed narratives, beyond internalized inferiority, beyond the fatigue caused by racism. To illuminate the spirit is to restore clarity, dignity, balance, and purpose.

Equally important is the principle of *Ma'at*—truth, balance, harmony, reciprocity, and justice. From this perspective, Black fatigue is not simply emotional exhaustion; it is the consequence of living in systems that routinely violate Ma'at. Healing is an active recommitment to truth and balance within ourselves and our communities, even when external systems resist or even deny the validity of those values.

Part IV, Building a Sustainable Future, looks beyond survival toward legacy. It explores what it means to create systems, communities, and cultures that will thrive for generations to come and presents somatic systems change models such as those offered by Resmaa Menakem, which posit that communities and institutions have collective nervous systems that can be dysregulated by racism and chronic stress.

How Is *Healing Black Fatigue* Different?

Table 1 offers a summary of what this book is and is not, to help you understand our intentions and what to expect from the journey ahead.

Table 1. What this book is and is not

THIS BOOK *IS* . . .	THIS BOOK *IS NOT* . . .
A companion to *Black Fatigue* that moves from naming harm to exploring restoration	A repetition of trauma narratives without pathways for renewal
Grounded in African-centered psychology, ancestral and Indigenous wisdom, and communal healing traditions	Limited to Western psychological or clinical models
About acknowledging Black fatigue as systemic, cumulative, intergenerational, embodied, and spiritual	A framing of fatigue as individual burnout, stress, or personal weakness
Designed to support restoration, renewal, resistance, and joy simultaneously	A call to "cope better" or be more resilient

THIS BOOK *IS* . . .	THIS BOOK *IS NOT* . . .
Intergenerational by design, reflecting elder wisdom and next-generation leadership	Written from a single generational or professional perspective
Rooted in global and diasporic perspectives on Black identity and healing	Limited to a US-centric or narrow cultural lens
A book that honors reflection and practice without being a workbook	A prescriptive, step-by-step manual or checklist for healing
Explicit about the role of systems, policies, and institutions in producing fatigue	A book that individualizes harm or places responsibility for healing solely on the reader
Accessible across life stages, roles, and settings (families, communities, workplaces)	Written only for clinicians, activists, or academic audiences
An invitation to remember, realign, and reclaim identity	A demand to arrive at a fixed or singular definition of identity
Informed by Sakhu (illumination of the spirit) and Ma'at (truth, balance, harmony)	Detached from spiritual, ancestral, or ethical grounding
A book that treats joy and rest as rights, not rewards	A narrative that glorifies resilience or normalizes depletion
Honest about grief, anger, and fatigue without romanticizing suffering	Rooted in forced optimism that dismisses the reality of Black fatigue

This book does not ask readers to endure injustice more gracefully. It asks what becomes possible when healing is treated as restoration and when fatigue is understood as a collective signal rather than a personal, inevitable condition.

Black Fatigue names what is happening to us. *Healing Black Fatigue* provides choices to respond with more intention, more clarity, and more care.

Part I

RECLAIMING YOUR IDENTITY

Se wo were fi na wosan kofa a yenkyiri.

It is not taboo to go back and fetch what you forgot (or left behind).

—Akan proverb (Ghana)

ONE

WHO AM I? EXPLORING YOUR IDENTITY

Know whence you came.
If you know whence you came, there is really no limit to where you can go.

—James Baldwin, American writer and civil rights activist[1]

On the surface, "Who am I?" may seem like an easy question until you start to peel back the layers of your identity. You might simply start with your name, then recognize that within that name is a lineage that begins with your parents and goes back many generations. If you are of African descent, it is likely that somewhere in that line, you come from people who were at one time enslaved. And if enslavement is a part of your ancestry, it is also likely that there are fractures in your family tree due to families being savagely torn apart.

Healing begins with knowing (perhaps discovering) who you are and learning to love yourself unconditionally. Pride can come from researching your lineage and discovering who your ancestors were, what they did, and how these familial connections have shaped you. In recognition of this, in recent years there has been a growing movement of African diasporans, particularly Black Americans, traveling to Africa as part of a broader search for identity, connection, and belonging. "Roots travel"—trips motivated by shared ethnic heritage and race—is one of the fastest-growing segments of the travel industry.[2]

These actions constitute a beginning to your identity exploration. There is so much more, which we will discuss throughout Part I of this book.

REFLECTION

- How much do you know about your ancestors?
- Have you explored your DNA through sources like African Ancestry?[3]
- What conversations have you had with your elders about your heritage?
- Why might it be important to your sense of wholeness and wellness to explore your lineage?
- How much energy do you have to do this type of exploration? (Be honest!)
- If you have experienced roots travel, what was it like for you? Did it support your self-awareness?

Identity and the Original Disruption

As we explore the answer to the question "Who am I?" it is important to acknowledge how, for people of African descent, that understanding was intentionally and systematically disrupted through the trafficking of enslaved Africans during the transatlantic slave trade. Beginning in the early 1500s and lasting for more than 350 years, this forced migration—one of the largest and most violent in human history—removed an estimated 12.5 million Africans from their homelands. Of those, approximately

10.7 million survived the Middle Passage between 1526 and 1867, arriving in the Americas and the Caribbean to be sold into slavery.[4]

This was a deliberate severing of people from family, language, culture, spirituality, land, and lineage.

African societies were composed of nations, ethnic groups, clans, and kinship systems. People knew who they were in relation to ancestors and descendants, to land and community. Identity was collective, relational, and deeply rooted. The slave trade destroyed that rich history.

Families were routinely separated at every stage of the process—during capture, at coastal holding forts, aboard slave ships, and again at auction blocks in the Americas. Children were torn from parents. Siblings were sold to different plantations. Partners were intentionally separated to prevent collective resistance. Names were changed and replaced with those assigned by the enslavers. Languages were suppressed. Spiritual practices were criminalized. Lineage was intentionally denied.

In many parts of the Americas, laws reinforced this form of epistemicide. Identity dislocation was legalized under *partus sequitur ventrem*, adopted in British colonies in the mid-1600s, under which a child's legal status followed that of the mother. This ensured the perpetual enslavement of generations while simultaneously destabilizing traditional African family structures. Black families were denied legal recognition, protection, or permanence.[5] While formal enslavement had been abolished in most parts of the world by the mid-19th century, the deleterious effects persist to the present day, as discussed in Chapter 3 of this book and in *Black Fatigue*.

In March 2026, the United Nations (UN) General Assembly adopted a resolution led by Ghana declaring "the trafficking of enslaved Africans and racialized chattel enslavement of Africans as the gravest crime against humanity."[6] The resolution, signed by 123 members, asks nations to pursue reparatory justice, including formal apologies, restitution, and compensation. It also demands the return of cultural artifacts, such as artworks, monuments, and national archives, to their countries of origin. Three countries—the United

States, Israel, and Argentina— voted against the resolution, and all twenty-seven countries representing the European Union (EU) abstained. It is not clear what impact the resolution will have, but it is a start in acknowledging the historical wrongs and their lasting effects across the diaspora.

From "Who Are You?" to "Who Do You Belong To?"

One of the most profound impacts of enslavement was the shift from identity to objectification. Enslaved Africans were not recognized as whole humans with histories and futures; they were reduced to property, units of labor, and economic assets. The question asked was no longer "Who are you?" but "What are you worth, and who do you belong to?"

This reduction of humanity has had a profound impact across generations.

Reclaiming our identity is critical to healing. African-centered psychology, which we introduce in more detail in Chapter 2, teaches us the self is not merely individual, but extended—connected to ancestors, community, and cultural memory. When those connections are violently disrupted, the effects do not disappear with legislated emancipation.

After the formal abolition of slavery across the Americas, the work of identity restoration was never supported at the structural level. Instead, Black communities across the globe were met with new systems of control: Black Codes, convict leasing, Jim Crow laws, colonial governance, and racial apartheid. The laws might have changed, but the assault on identity continued.

Black people were expected to assimilate into societies that denied their humanity while simultaneously being told their cultural ways were inferior, dangerous, or irrelevant. And many of those perceptions persist today, worsening Black fatigue.

The Inheritance of Disrupted Identity

Today, many Black people carry questions of identity that feel deeply personal and are historically rooted.

REFLECTION

- Do you think of yourself as African, African American, Caribbean, Afro-Latinx, Black, or something else entirely?
- Who gets to define who you are?
- To what extent do you allow others to define you?

These questions are not signs of confusion. They are the consequences of forced disconnection.

Black fatigue often emerges when individuals are asked, explicitly or implicitly, to define themselves in environments that do not acknowledge this history. In African-centered psychology terms, when people are expected to be whole without this context, this is a condition of misalignment. The spirit recognizes the rupture even when the mind has been taught to normalize it. You will find more on the idea of restoring alignment in Chapter 2.

Our Memories Are Carried in the Body

What the transatlantic slave trade could not fully destroy was the memory we all carry in our bodies: values embedded in community and wisdom passed down through adaptation. New cultures emerged—African American, Afro-Caribbean, Afro-Brazilian—out of survival and creativity under unimaginable oppression.

Identity did not vanish; it transformed.

Music, storytelling, spirituality, food, humor, and resistance became vessels for continuity. Even in conditions designed to erase ancestry, Black people created meaning, belonging, and connection.

William Cross's Model of Black Identity Formation (the Nigrescence Model)

Given the intentional attempts to reframe the identity of people of African descent in negative ways, psychologist William E. Cross Jr.

developed one of the most influential frameworks for understanding Black identity development, commonly known as the Nigrescence model (from the French *nigrescence*, meaning the process of becoming Black).[7] First introduced in the early 1970s and refined over several decades, the model describes how Black identity evolves in response to personal experience, social context, and exposure to racism.

Rather than viewing identity as fixed, Cross emphasized that Black identity is dynamic, shaped by historical forces, lived experiences, and conscious meaning-making.

The model outlines five stages of identity development. It is important to note that these stages are not strictly linear, nor does everyone experience them in the same way.

STAGE 1: PRE-ENCOUNTER

The initial stage is characterized by an individual's limited awareness of their racial identity and the influence of societal norms that perpetuate systemic racism, sometimes viewing themselves as "colorblind" or "just American." At this stage, individuals may adopt mainstream ideals and disassociate from their cultural roots, frequently unaware of the impact on their self-perception.

This stage often reflects the success of societal conditioning. In contexts where Black identity has historically been stigmatized, distancing oneself from one's cultural roots can function as a survival strategy.

STAGE 2: ENCOUNTER

The encounter stage is marked by a disruptive experience, often an incident of racism, exclusion, or injustice that challenges previously held beliefs about race and belonging. This moment creates cognitive and emotional dissonance.

Encounters can be sudden (a traumatic event) or cumulative (a realization that patterns of inequity are not accidental). They force a reckoning with race as a meaningful factor in one's life. Many people may first begin to consciously feel Black fatigue at this stage, when awareness sharpens and the denial of systemic racism becomes impossible.

Mary-Frances remembers:

I entered the encounter stage for the first time at age five, in kindergarten, when a white boy called the only other Black child in the class and me the N-word. We were not familiar with the word, but we knew that it was not nice by the way he said it, and we both started crying. I had limited awareness of my racial identity before this encounter. It was very confusing and traumatic as such a young child to come to the realization that someone might not like me because of the color of my skin. When I tell this story to Black colleagues and friends, many share that their encounter experience also happened at a young age.

Mareisha recalls:

The first time I remember noticing a difference due to race was when I was in the sixth grade. I went to a predominantly white school and recall my classmates being fascinated by my hair. Black people's hair tends to be more coily or kinky, whereas white people's hair is straighter. I would get relaxers frequently to straighten my hair, but as any Black person who has had a relaxer knows, it only stays straight for so long, and as your hair grows out, you have a mix of straight hair at the ends and coily toward the roots. Because of that, I was able to make my hair stand straight up without it falling. The kids in my class would often ask me to make my bangs stick up. At the time, I didn't take offense, and I am not sure if they meant any malice. Looking back, this is the first time I remember being othered.

STAGE 3: IMMERSION/EMERSION

In the immersion phase of this stage, individuals may actively seek connection to Black culture, history, and community while questioning and rejecting dominant cultural values that previously defined success or belonging. This period can involve anger, grief, pride, or intense emotional energy as identity is reclaimed.

The emersion phase reflects a softening, moving from reaction toward reflection, allowing space for nuance, complexity, and integration.

This stage can be both energizing and exhausting. While reclaiming identity can be affirming, without meaningful support, the emotional intensity of confronting historical and contemporary harm can deepen fatigue.

STAGE 4: INTERNALIZATION

Here, Black identity becomes integrated, secure, and self-defined. Individuals are less reactive to external validation or invalidation and more grounded in their own values. Blackness is affirmed without requiring opposition or defensiveness.

Identity at this stage supports psychological well-being, flexibility, and resilience. While internalization can reduce some aspects of fatigue by restoring agency and self-trust, it does not eliminate exposure to systemic harm.

STAGE 5: INTERNALIZATION/COMMITMENT

In the final stage, identity is linked to purpose and responsibility. Individuals often feel a commitment to social justice, community uplift, mentorship, or structural change. Black identity becomes not only personal but relational and collective. While this stage can be deeply meaningful, it also introduces the risk of activism fatigue or leadership exhaustion if care, boundaries, and communal support are not maintained—topics we explore throughout the book.

Cross's model frames the exploration of identity as developmental, normal, and not pathological. There is not something wrong with us for struggling with identity and not being able to easily answer the question "Who am I?" given the oppressive history of anti-Black racism. It also highlights the emotional labor involved in developing a positive, grounded self-concept in a racialized world.

This model helps us understand the psychological stages of Black identity formation. African-centered psychology, which we explore in depth in Chapter 2, extends this understanding by showing us that identity is not only developed, but also remembered, restored, and realigned through community, ancestry, and spirit.

Reclaiming Identity as Healing

Healing Black fatigue begins, in part, with reclaiming the right to define oneself beyond imposed narratives, beyond survival, beyond limitations. It begins with acknowledging that identity disruption has a history, and that confusion, longing, and fragmentation are not personal failures but consequences of that history. It also helps to understand how Black identity is formed in a racialized world, as William Cross's model shows us.

To ask "Who am I?" is to begin the work of restoration. To explore identity is to resist erasure and to connect to ancestry, community, and shared values.

This process is not about arriving at a fixed identity. It is about remembering that you have the right to ask, to discover, and to reclaim who you are on your own terms, in your own time, and in relationship with others.

The "I Am From" poem is used in classrooms and workplace training throughout the world.[8] Rooted in a study of personal identity, it can help one reflect on one's ancestors and culture, and how and where one belongs. We present a template here. Try it if it resonates with you, and customize it as you see fit.

We also include here an example of a completed poem, authored by Valda Valbrun, CEO of The Valbrun Consulting Group and a senior consultant for The Winters Group (used with permission).

"I AM FROM" POEM

I am from ______________________________
(specific ordinary item)

From ________________ and ________________
(product name) *(product name)*

I am from the ______________________________
(home description)

________________, ________________, ________________
(adjective) *(adjective)* *(sensory detail)*

I am from ______________________________,
(plant, flower, natural item)

____
(description of above item)

I'm from ________________ and ________________
(family tradition) *(family trait)*

From ________________ and ________________
(name of family member) *(another family name)*

I'm from the ________________ and ________________
(description of family tendency) *(another one)*

From ________________ and ________________
(something you were told as a child) *(another)*

I'm from ________________, ________________
(representation of religion or lack of) *(further description)*

I'm from ______________________________
(place of birth and family ancestry)

________________, ________________
(a food item that represents your family) *(another one)*

From the ______________________________
(family story about a specific person and detail)

The ______________________________
(another detail about another family member)

____
(location of family pictures, mementos, archives)

____
(line explaining the importance of family items)

I AM FROM . . .

I am from Austrel and Marie-Denise's sacrifices.

I am from immigrant work ethic and "leave everything you touch, better than you found it."

I am from a hyphenated life; Haitian-American, "diri kole ak pwa" (Haitian red beans and rice) at home and grilled cheese sandwiches at school.

I am from the loneliness of only-ness; the only one of my siblings born in the United States, the only Black kid at that Catholic School, and the only adult of color as Principal of that middle school.

I am a mother, a daughter, a sister, an aunt, a teacher, a leader.

I am from "you're pretty for a dark-skinned girl" to owning the meaning of my name.

I am Valda: powerful, a ruler, a warrior.

I am from resilient people, who stand tall despite disasters.

I am from sitting in the sacrifices of many, and I honor them each and every day as I give back to the world.

REFLECTION

- When you ask "Who am I?" what answers come most easily? Which feel more complicated?
- Where are you on William Cross's model of Black identity formation?
- What parts of your identity feel inherited? What parts feel imposed?
- Where and when do you feel most whole? Most fragmented?

(continued)

- Who are the people, living or remembered, who shaped your sense of self?
- What messages about Black identity did you receive growing up, spoken or unspoken?
- What aspects of yourself feel whole and natural when you are not "performing" or explaining who you are?
- What does loving yourself unconditionally look like? Feel like?

Summary

Answering the question "Who am I?" is often more complex for people of African descent, shaped by histories of displacement, enslavement, and imposed identity. For generations, African people were stripped of their names, cultures, family ties, and ways of knowing, and were forced to assume identities defined by enslavers and racial hierarchies. Even after the legal abolition of slavery, new laws and social systems emerged that continued to criminalize, dehumanize, and distort Black identity.

Reflecting on who we are and how history has shaped that understanding is essential to healing Black fatigue. Identity is not a fixed label. It is something that has been disrupted and can be restored. Researching one's roots, reclaiming the right to self-definition beyond imposed narratives, and embracing the concept of the extended self are foundational steps in cultivating self-awareness. Through this process, identity shifts from something imposed and defined by dominant culture to something rooted in your truth and connection to your culture, restoring you to wholeness.

TWO

FINDING ONESELF THROUGH AFRICAN-CENTERED PSYCHOLOGY AND INDIGENOUS WISDOM

Our ancestors have prepared the way for us to be, Divine Spirit Beings, living in a reality of spirit, called to enlighten, restore, and heal.

—Wade W. Nobles, founding member,
Association of Black Psychologists[1]

William Cross's model of Black identity development, introduced in Chapter 1, teaches us that identity is shaped by environment, social mirrors, and historical narratives. African-centered psychology provides a more holistic way of understanding and unpacking these influences for people of African descent. African-centered psychology is philosophically different from Eurocentric or Western psychology. At the most fundamental level, these approaches diverge in their assumptions about what it means to be human, how knowledge is formed, and what constitutes well-being.

Eurocentric psychology emerged from Enlightenment traditions that prioritize rationalism, individualism, materialism, and the separation of mind from body and spirit.[2] In this worldview, the individual is treated as autonomous, self-contained, and primarily responsible for managing distress, often without acknowledging historical context or collective harms. Although this is the dominant model in academic and clinical psychology, it is not representative of the vast majority of the global population.[3]

In 2010, three cultural psychologists published a paper entitled "The Weirdest People in the World?" introducing the acronym WEIRD (Western, Educated, Industrialized, Rich, and Democratic) to describe the subjects most studied in human psychology.[4] The researchers maintain that members of WEIRD societies, who accounted for approximately 96 percent of subjects in behavior science research during the years they surveyed, are "among the least representative populations one could find for generalizing about humans." The pool these subjects are drawn from represents only about 12 percent of the world's population, and they are often statistical outliers in areas like social behavior, moral reasoning, and visual perception.

Approximately 85 percent of the world's population are Black, Asian, Brown, Indigenous, Latinx, or of mixed heritage.[5] Yet despite being the Global Majority, they not an integral part of psychological research; instead, assumptions, theories, diagnoses, and generalizations are made based on the WEIRD "outliers." Of course, Eurocentric psychology is not monolithic; it includes humanistic, relational, liberation-oriented, and community approaches. However, scholars have consistently noted that dominant Western psychological frameworks, especially as institutionalized in clinical training, diagnostics, and workplace wellness, often reflect assumptions that African-centered psychology fundamentally challenges.

As indicated in Table 2, African-centered psychology begins from a radically different premise than Eurocentric psychology: that human beings are relational, spiritual, and communal by nature, and that identity, health, and meaning cannot be separated from ancestry, culture, ethics, and collective responsibility.

Table 2. African-centered versus Eurocentric psychology[6]

DIMENSION	AFRICAN-CENTERED PSYCHOLOGY	EUROCENTRIC (WESTERN) PSYCHOLOGY
Foundational worldview	Rooted in African belief systems emphasizing interconnectedness, spirituality, and collective responsibility	Rooted in Enlightenment traditions emphasizing rationalism, empiricism, and individualism
View of the self	Extended self, identity connected to ancestors, community, spirit, and future generations	Individual self, autonomous, bounded, self-contained
Role of culture	Foundational to meaning, identity, and wellness	Treated as a variable or "competency" added to a dominant norm
Spirituality	Central to psychological health; spirit (Sakhu) is foundational	Often excluded or treated as separate from psychology
View of trauma	Collective, historical, intergenerational, and embodied	Often individualized and event-based
Relationship to power and history	Explicitly centers racism, colonization, and oppression	Structural power imbalances are minimized or ignored
Goal of healing	Focuses on restoration, illumination, liberation, alignment, wholeness	Focuses on diagnosis and symptom reduction
Role of community	A primary site of healing and regulation	Often viewed as secondary to individual treatment
Knowledge sources	Ancestral wisdom, lived experience, oral tradition, spirituality, scholarship	Empirical research privileging Western norms
Identity	Ancestral, to be remembered, reclaimed, and restored	Developed primarily through individual processes
Fatigue	Signals systemic and spiritual imbalances	Framed as the result of stress, burnout, or poor self-care
Orientation to justice	Healing and justice are inseparable; healing is resistance	Often considered outside of psychology's scope
Measures of wellness	Alignment, dignity, wholeness, relational harmony	Productivity, symptom reduction, self-reported functioning

In the African-centered worldview, well-being is inseparable from justice, culture is not an accessory but a foundation, and the illumination of the spirit is as essential as cognitive and emotional functioning. These foundational differences are key in understanding and healing Black fatigue, because a framework that isolates the individual cannot adequately address the exhaustion produced by collective, historical, systemic forces.

Psychologist Wade W. Nobles, a founding member of the Association of Black Psychologists and a leading authority on African-centered psychology, captures this perspective in his work, describing African psychology as concerned with the illumination and liberation of the spirit and the restoration of African people to their proper place in the human family.[7]

REFLECTION

- How were you taught to understand suffering and manage stress?
- When you seek professional help to support your physical and mental well-being, how much attention is given to historical and collective harms as possible underlying forces?
- Do you feel that your support system reflects a holistic, African-centered approach to healing and well-being? (See Chapter 9.)

Sakhu and Ma'at, integral parts of African-centered psychology, call forth ancestral practices to help us heal Black fatigue.

Sakhu: Illumination of Spirit as a Healing Framework

In African-centered psychology, Sakhu (often discussed by Nobles in the form Sakhu Djaer/Skh Djr) is the illumination and liberation of the spirit. Nobles describes Sakhu scholarship as "the deep, profound . . . search, study, understanding and mastery of the illumination of the human spirit," grounded in the premise that a full understanding of reality acknowledges spirit as the basis of what is known and knowable.[8] Here, spirit is understood as the animating life force that connects the individual to ancestors, community, purpose, and one's very existence. According to Nobles, *spiritness* (spirit) is distinct from *spirituality*: Spiritness is the condition of being spirit (i.e., humans are first and foremost spirit; reality is spirit), and spirituality is the quality of being spiritual.[9] He maintains that spiritness is more related to metaphysics than religion.

African belief systems would posit that the process of knowing comes more from spirit than the mind. In this worldview, identity is not limited to roles, labels, or external achievements; it is anchored in an inner knowing of *being*—a sense of who one is at the deepest level. When spirit is ignored, suppressed, or fractured, identity becomes unstable and overly dependent on external validation. This spiritual disconnection is a significant contributor to Black fatigue, as individuals are forced to navigate hostile environments without access to the full grounding of their spiritual selves. Restoring spirit through remembrance, alignment, and illumination strengthens identity, reduces fragmentation, and supports a sense of wholeness that endures beyond circumstance.

In his seminal essay tracing African (Black) psychology's development, Nobles calls for a Pan-African psychology explicitly founded on spirit/Sakhu, underscoring that African-centered healing is not simply symptom reduction but restoration of inner clarity, meaning, and wholeness.[10]

While Sakhu draws on ancient African philosophies, it can be practiced today by reducing the dominance of external evaluation (e.g., the white gaze), cultivating quiet moments of discernment, and returning to inner truth through breath, embodied awareness, prayer/meditation, ancestral remembering, and community witness. In daily life, Sakhu becomes a discipline of asking: What is true beneath the noise? What restores my inner coherence? What reconnects me to purpose and spirit? This shift directly counters Black fatigue's fragmentation by restoring the self to clarity and spiritual grounding.

Ma'at: Truth, Balance, and Ethical Alignment as a Daily Practice

Ma'at originated in ancient Kemet (Egypt) as both a goddess and a comprehensive moral cosmic principle representing truth, justice, rightness, order, balance, and harmony—a standard understood to hold society together and restrain chaos. Scholars note that Ma'at was foundational to Egyptian social life and law, expressing the "correct order and balance of the universe" and functioning as an ethical mandate rather than a personal virtue.[11] In modern African-centered ethics, Ma'at can be thought of as the ethical counterpart to Sakhu: If Sakhu restores spiritual clarity, Ma'at restores alignment—the commitment to live in right relationship with self and others.[12]

Practicing Ma'at today can be translated into everyday choices: telling the truth (including naming harm accurately), pursuing balance (work/rest, giving/receiving), insisting on reciprocity (refusing double standards), and choosing actions that preserve dignity and harmony rather than performance. In workplaces, Ma'at may take the form of boundaries (which we discuss in more detail in Chapters 5 and 6), documentation, principled speech, and restorative repair; in personal life, it may look like repairing relationships, releasing internalized oppression, and building routines that protect equilibrium. It is not abstract philosophy. It is a daily standard of "rightness" drawing upon ancestral wisdom that supports sustainable wellness, because it challenges the conditions that produce Black fatigue: chronic injustice, perpetual vigilance, and the normalization of imbalance. We share an example of how to practice Ma'at in Chapter 8.

Spirit, Identity, and Healing

Across Indigenous traditions worldwide, healing is understood as the restoration of right relationship within the self, with others, with ancestors, and with the natural world. While these belief systems arise from distinct cultures and histories, as shown in Table 3 at the end of this chapter, they converge around shared principles that stand in contrast to Eurocentric individualistic models of wellness. As we discussed earlier, African and Indigenous worldviews are actually held by most of the Global Majority. Their marginalization by the dominant culture is not a matter of numbers or efficacy but of power, specifically the historical and ongoing normalization of Eurocentric frameworks through colonialism, institutional authority, economic control, and global sociopolitical systems of influence.

REFLECTION

- To what extent have you embraced Eurocentric ways of knowing and being? How has that served you?
- Which of your beliefs and practices emerged from African-centered and Indigenous belief systems?
- When you think of spirit, what comes to mind?
- What are some times when you have felt a true connection to spirit?
- Spirit is different from spirituality. How do you think about them differently?

Summary

African-centered psychology offers a different and, for some readers, new framework for deepening self-awareness and answering the enduring question, "Who am I?" In contrast to Eurocentric psychological traditions that often emphasize individualism and adaptation, African-centered psychology and Indigenous beliefs are communal, relational, and grounded in ancestral wisdom. Recalling ancient African understandings of spirit (Sakhu) and ethical alignment (Ma'at) returns identity to a more human and cultural context. From this foundation, the work of healing Black fatigue can begin—not as self-correction, but as restoration.

Table 3. African and Indigenous views of spirit, identity, and healing

DIMENSION	AFRICAN	NATIVE AMERICAN/ INDIGENOUS NORTH AMERICAN	INDIGENOUS LATIN AMERICAN/ MESOAMERICAN	INDIGENOUS SOUTH AMERICAN	ASIAN (EAST, SOUTHEAST, SOUTH)
Foundational view of the human being	Humans are spiritual, communal, and relational; identity is extended.	Humans exist within a sacred web of relations (people, land, ancestors).	Humans are embedded in collective, spiritual, and ecological systems.	Humans are participants in an animated, relational cosmos.	Humans are relational beings embedded in family, community, and moral order.
Role of spirit	Illumination and liberation of spirit are core to healing.	Spirit animates all life; sacred and everyday are inseparable.	Spirit and material life are unified.	Spirit is present in humans, ancestors, and nature.	Spirit (*chi*, *khwan*, *semangat*, *prana*) animates life and well-being.
Understanding of identity	Identity is ancestral, communal, and historical; the self is extended.	Identity is shaped by clan, tribe, lineage, and responsibility.	Identity is rooted in extended family and community.	Identity is formed through kinship, land, and ancestry.	Identity is shaped through family lineage, social roles, and moral relationships.
View of family	Family includes ancestors, elders, community, and future generations.	Family includes clan systems and elders.	*Familia ampliada* (extended family) is central.	Caregiving is shared across kin and community.	Strong intergenerational structures emphasize filial responsibility.
Time orientation	Time is cyclical and ancestral.	Time is circular; emphasis on continuity.	Cyclical rhythms are tied to land and ritual.	Time is seasonal and cyclical.	Time is cyclical; impermanence and continuity coexist.

DIMENSION	AFRICAN	NATIVE AMERICAN/ INDIGENOUS NORTH AMERICAN	INDIGENOUS LATIN AMERICAN/ MESOAMERICAN	INDIGENOUS SOUTH AMERICAN	ASIAN (EAST, SOUTHEAST, SOUTH)
Understanding of distress	Distress reflects spiritual, relational, or moral misalignment.	Distress reflects disharmony in the relational web.	Distress reflects imbalance in person–community–nature relationships.	Distress reflects disruption of harmony.	Distress reflects imbalance of mind, body, spirit, and relationships.
Relationship to nature	Humans are spiritually connected to nature.	Land is sacred and relational.	Harmony with nature is essential.	Nature is alive and relational.	Humans are part of an interconnected natural order.
Approach to healing	Restoration of spirit, identity, and balance.	Ceremony, elders, storytelling, communal ritual.	Balance, reciprocity, ritual, community care.	Ceremony, plant knowledge, communal healing.	Mindfulness, ritual, community harmony, moral realignment.
Ethical orientation	Ma'at: truth, balance, justice, reciprocity.	Right relationship and respect.	Reciprocity and collective well-being (*Buen Vivir*).	Balance, respect, responsibility.	Moral harmony (*dharma*, *metta*, *adat*).
Purpose of life	Alignment with spirit, community, and moral order.	Living in balance with all living beings.	Collective well-being.	Maintaining cosmic and social harmony.	Cultivating harmony, compassion, and balance.
What heals fatigue	Reconnection to spirit, ancestry, community, truth.	Restoration of belonging and harmony.	Collective care and balance.	Realignment with land and community.	Stillness, ethical living, communal grounding.

THREE

FAMILY, BELONGING, AND IDENTITY

Umuntu ngumuntu ngabantu.

A person is a person through other people.

—Zulu/Xhosa proverb (South Africa)

In Chapter 2, we contrasted African-centered psychology and African and Indigenous ideologies related to human existence with those that originated from European Enlightenment beliefs. One of the primary differences is how the individual is thought of. In African and Indigenous cultures, identity is inseparable from the concept of the extended self. From this perspective, the self does not end at the boundaries of the individual body or ego but is inherently connected to family, community, ancestors, culture, spirituality, and future generations. Identity is not formed solely through personal choice or individual achievement; rather, it emerges through relationships and legacy. Who we are is shaped by who came before us, who surrounds us, and who will come after us.

Identity as the Extended Self

Embracing the concept of identity as extending beyond the individual stands in contrast to Eurocentric models that frame it as a personal possession, constructed primarily through internal traits or narratives and shaped only by one's own experiences. When identity is disconnected from the extended self—as has occurred through enslavement, colonization, and forced assimilation—people feel, consciously or subconsciously, the fragmentation it creates. African-centered and Indigenous ideologies recognize this severing as a source of profound psychological and spiritual misalignment.

Black fatigue often reflects not only external stress, but the burden of navigating life without the full relational scaffolding that affirms identity and belonging. Reconnecting identity to the extended self restores grounding. It reinforces that one's worth is not contingent on external validation, that meaning is collective rather than solitary, and that healing occurs most fully when identity is remembered and lived in relationship. We share some specific ways to enhance the healing process through remembering and relationships in Part III.

Proverbs often reflect the psychological assumptions of a culture. Across African, Indigenous, and non-Western traditions, identity is understood as relational and collective, while Eurocentric traditions tend to emphasize autonomy and self-reliance as measures of worth and success.

Table 4 displays common idioms that help us understand the different worldviews.

Table 4. Proverbs to understand worldviews about "self"

CULTURAL TRADITION	REPRESENTATIVE PROVERBS/SAYINGS	CORE WORLDVIEW ON SELF AND BELONGING
Eurocentric/ Western	"Pull yourself up by your bootstraps." "Every person for themselves." "You make your own destiny."	The self is autonomous and self-contained. Success, failure, and responsibility are primarily individual. Belonging is conditional and often earned through performance or achievement.

CULTURAL TRADITION	REPRESENTATIVE PROVERBS/SAYINGS	CORE WORLDVIEW ON SELF AND BELONGING
African	"I am because we are" (*Ubuntu*). "One finger cannot lift a pebble." "The child who is not embraced by the village will burn it down to feel its warmth." "If you want to go fast, go alone. If you want to go far, go together."	The self is extended—rooted in family, community, ancestors, and future generations. Identity and survival are collective, and well-being depends on shared responsibility and care.
Native American/ Indigenous North American	"We are all related" (*Mitákuye Oyás'iŋ*). "The frog does not drink up the pond in which it lives." "A people without a history is like wind over buffalo grass."	Identity is relational and sacred, grounded in kinship, land, ancestors, and community. Individual actions are evaluated by their impact on the whole.
South American Indigenous (Andean, Amazonian)	"One hand does not wash itself." "No one eats alone." "The community is the heart; the individual is the pulse."	Well-being is collective, not private. Harmony, reciprocity, and balance (*Buen Vivir/ Sumak Kawsay*) are valued over accumulation or individual advancement.
Asian (East, Southeast, South)	"The world is one family" (*Vasudhaiva Kutumbakam*). "A single bamboo breaks easily; a bundle is strong." "The family is the root of the nation."	The self is nested within family, lineage, and moral obligation. Harmony, duty, and collective stability take precedence over personal preference or individual gain.

When individualism is imposed on cultures rooted in collective identity, the result is often fatigue from trying to fit into systems that are unnatural rather than empowering.

REFLECTION

- To what extent were you taught to embrace more of the Eurocentric proverbs as your truth?
- How have African-centered and Indigenous ways of being influenced you?
- Where and when might you have experienced conflicts between the two?
- What does the concept of the extended self mean to you? How do you live it?

Family and Identity

As discussed in Chapter 1, the trafficking of enslaved Africans during the transatlantic slave trade systematically dismantled family systems, severed lineage, and effectively criminalized African ways of organizing life. Black family bonds were rendered legally irrelevant, and children inherited the status of slave through their mothers. By design, this created conditions where familial belonging was destabilized. Western psychology later embraced the idea of the nuclear family, a framework that viewed Black family structures through a deficit lens, despite the fact that they were shaped by forced dismantling.

The concept of the nuclear family—a household consisting of two parents and their children, economically and socially independent from extended kin—is considered universal and natural by Western standards. In reality, it is a historically specific social arrangement, shaped by European industrialization, capitalism, and Protestant moral traditions.

Sociologists and historians trace the rise of the nuclear family to Western Europe and North America in the 18th and 19th centuries, when economic production shifted from agrarian and communal systems to wage labor and private households.[1] Within this framework, adulthood is defined by independence and self-sufficiency. Caregiving for the elderly is often outsourced, and responsibility for survival rests primarily on the individual household. Extended family, elders, and community networks are considered secondary. These conditions are reflected in Western psychology, which tends to frame psychological maturity as separation from the nuclear family and identity as based on individual achievement.[2]

For people of African descent whose lineage and ways of life, rooted in extended kinship and communal responsibility, had been destroyed by the transatlantic slave trade, this model simply did not fit. Enslaved Africans were denied legal marriage. Children were routinely separated from their parents, and caregiving was violently interrupted. Yet, when the nuclear family later emerged as the norm and ideal, Black families were judged and regulated according to a standard they had been deliberately prevented from forming.[3]

In the late 19th and 20th centuries, US social policy and social science often framed Black families as "deviant" for relying on extended kin, friends, and communal caregiving, which were precisely the strategies that had enabled survival during enslavement.[4] Rather than recognizing these arrangements as both necessary and culturally grounded, dominant frameworks pathologized them through deficit narratives that equated "normal" with conformity to the nuclear model.

African-centered and Indigenous understandings of family extend far beyond the nuclear household. Family includes elders, cousins, godparents, neighbors, mentors, and community members who share responsibility for care, guidance, and socialization. And these cultural norms often influence living arrangements. According to 2021 data, in the United States Black (17 percent), Asian (14 percent), and Latino (14 percent) families are much more likely to live in intergenerational homes compared to non-Hispanic whites (7 percent).[5] These arrangements are driven by cultural traditions, economic necessity, and, for some, immigration patterns. They are natural and normal for communal-based cultures, even though they might seem abnormal by Eurocentric standards.

Another example of the extended family concept beyond living arrangements is how many Black people refer to one another as *sister*, *brother*, *auntie*, and so on when there is no biological tie, or use terms like *play cousin* to signal kinship that is not contingent on bloodlines. These terms acknowledge recognition of shared humanity, mutual respect, and an unspoken understanding of our ancestral connection. In the same spirit, designations such as "brother-in-love" or "sister-in-love" rather than brother-in-law or sister-in-law reflect an African-centered orientation to relationship that prioritizes chosen connection over legal designation. Rather than emphasizing ownership or obligation, such language centers intentional belonging. It is also common for Black people to dispense with qualifiers like "half" or "step" to describe familial relationships.

Research consistently shows that extended kinship networks have been a primary source of resilience for Black families across generations, especially in the face of racist systems that continued to dismantle family structures. These networks have offered survival strategies in environments where the dominant formal systems have not put much effort into effectively integrating cultural norms different from the nuclear model.

As an example, family reunions have long been an important cultural practice among Black families, serving as intentional acts of reconnection after generations of forced separation. Scholars note that these gatherings often extend far beyond the nuclear family, bringing together cousins, elders, "chosen" kin, and multiple branches of lineage across regions and generations.[6] More than social events, Black family reunions function as living expressions of the extended family, reinforcing shared identity and history, honoring ancestors, restoring continuity, and inspiring joy. In this sense, they operate as communal healing practices, affirming belonging as assumed rather than earned and countering the fragmentation that has historically shaped Black family life.

When we lived in the Rochester, New York, suburb of Perinton in the 1980s, Black families were a rarity. Whenever we encountered another Black person, often simply passing each other in the grocery store, we instinctively exchanged greetings and contact information. These brief moments of recognition reflected an unspoken understanding of shared identity and the need for connection in spaces where we were not only in the numerical minority but often felt the white gaze.

Over time, these informal encounters evolved into the creation of the Perinton African American Heritage Committee (PAAHC). What began as a small group of families committed to honoring Black History Month grew into a vibrant, community-centered collective. Each year, we curated Black History Month celebrations that included original plays and musical performances, with both adults and children participating. Rehearsals began shortly after the Christmas holidays and rotated among our homes, turning living rooms into creative and communal spaces.

As the years passed, PAAHC expanded to include nearly three hundred people. Our Black History Month celebrations culminated in a community-wide soul food dinner that brought together families, friends, and allies of all racial and ethnic backgrounds from the Greater Rochester region to celebrate Black culture, history, and collective pride. Beyond Black History Month, we organized social gatherings and volunteer activities throughout the year, deepening friendships and reinforcing a sense of shared responsibility for one another.

For our family, PAAHC was more than an organization; it was a lived experience of extended family and belonging. It ensured that we had a clear sense of history, identity, and community. Although the formal group no longer exists, the relationships it fostered endure.

One such offshoot of PAAHC was a group we called "Sista Friends," originally composed of twelve professional Black women, most of us working in predominantly white environments. We met monthly to play Pokeno for pennies. These gatherings were not about the game; they were about connection. They provided a space free from the white gaze, where there was no need to code-switch, explain, or perform. Belonging was automatic. You were welcomed simply because you were you.

Those monthly gatherings were deeply healing. Even though many of us eventually relocated to different parts of the country, the bonds remained strong. We now reunite annually for a long weekend filled with laughter, rest, and renewal. These women are like sisters. We show up for one another in grief, surrounding each other with care during the loss of loved ones. We celebrate together as well, attending our children's graduations and weddings, sharing joy with the same depth and commitment as biological family.

These are just a few examples of how extended family and belonging function within Black communities. We encourage you to reflect on some of your own examples.

REFLECTION

- To what extent do you think of yourself as part of an extended family network that includes biological and non-biological members?
- Who is included in your extended family network? How do these people, individually and collectively, support you in your healing and sense of wholeness?
- In addition to family reunions, what are ways that you connect with extended family? How do these experiences enhance your sense of belonging?

Belonging and Identity

Belonging is increasingly recognized in psychological research as a core determinant of well-being. A sense of belonging has been linked to lower stress, improved mental health, greater resilience, and stronger identity coherence.[7] African-centered psychology has reflected these understandings for centuries, teaching that disconnection is harmful and that healing must involve reconnection to ancestors and other kin.

Black fatigue intensifies when belonging is uncertain or conditional. When we must constantly prove our worth, code-switch to be accepted, and navigate the isolation of predominantly white spaces, belonging can be elusive. African-centered psychology reframes this exhaustion as fatigue rooted in relational deprivation.

One setting where this uncertainty often manifests is in the workplace. The concept of "belonging" began to emerge as a distinct focus in this context relatively recently, as organizations expanded their approaches to diversity and inclusion. One influential voice in this shift was Pat Wadors, former chief human resources officer at LinkedIn, who spoke publicly about the need to integrate belonging into diversity initiatives and make it part of organizational strategy.[8] Other organizations embraced the idea, and DEIB (diversity, equity, inclusion, and belonging) became a common new way to think about diversity and inclusion.

While it is a noble aspiration, it is difficult, if not impossible, to achieve the type of belonging that heals Black fatigue through strategy. There are fundamental differences between organizational belonging and the birthright belonging rooted in African and Indigenous beliefs. Table 5 highlights some of these.

In focus groups conducted by The Winters Group with employees across companies and industries, Black and Brown workers consistently lament not feeling like they belong. You may feel safe to speak in meetings, but only if you code-switch. You may be encouraged to "bring your voice," but not your truth about how you feel excluded. You may be included, but only in ways that do not make the dominant group feel uncomfortable. This type of conditional belonging adds to Black fatigue.

Table 5. DEIB versus African-centered belonging

DEIB BELONGING IS . . .	AFRICAN-CENTERED BELONGING IS . . .
A feeling	Fundamental to existence; a state of being
Something organizations create; strategy; additive	Assumed and inherent, not needing to be created; one belongs because one *is*
Often tied to engagement, performance, or retention	Not a bonus or reward; a psychological and spiritual necessity
About inclusion within existing systems	About right relationship with extended family/the universe
About psychological safety and freedom from interpersonal punishment within specific contexts (e.g., the ability to speak freely)	About remaining whole, aligned, and connected in identity and spirit

Perhaps trying to find belonging in the workplace or other predominantly white spaces where it requires a great deal of emotional labor is not worth the effort. For Black people navigating racialized environments, knowing that you belong within the context of your ancestral roots and that you have a community outside the workplace where you are accepted as your authentic self can provide a buffer against the harmful effects of being in spaces where you feel that you do not fully belong. When identity and belonging are tied to deep, communal roots, external recognition and validation become less important.

Belonging requires being seen fully, without a need for constant explanation or fear of erasure.

Belonging cannot be created through strategy alone. It is shaped by the messages we receive about who belongs, who leads, who is protected, and who is expendable. This does not mean we should rely on idealized versions of family or community, because there are times when we may not feel a sense of belonging in those spaces either. It means intentionally cultivating spaces, relationships, practices, and rituals where belonging is unconditional.

Restoring Belonging

There are many formal and informal organizations and efforts that help Black people experience a true sense of belonging—the type envisioned by our ancestors, unconditional and creating a sense of wholeness.

Few institutions have played a more central role in sustaining Black identity and belonging than the Black church. Emerging during enslavement and evolving through Reconstruction, Jim Crow, the civil rights movement, and beyond, the Black church has functioned simultaneously as spiritual refuge, social center, political hub, and cultural anchor.[9]

Black fraternities and sororities, founded largely in the early 20th century in response to racial exclusion from white institutions, offer another example of African-centered belonging. While activity in white collegiate fraternal organizations often ends upon graduation, Black sororities and fraternities are lifelong kinship networks rooted in service, with post-graduate chapters that remain just as active around the world.

Other organizations also sustain this sense of belonging. Jack and Jill of America, founded in 1938, supports Black children and families, with a strong emphasis on collective parenting and community uplift. The Links, Incorporated, founded in 1946, is an international organization of professional Black women dedicated to service, leadership, and advocacy through programs that strengthen families, communities, and cultural heritage.

Prince Hall Freemasonry was founded in the late 18th century, when Black men were barred from white Masonic lodges. These lodges provided more than ritual and fellowship; they functioned as extended family systems, offering mutual aid and community protection during slavery, Reconstruction, and Jim Crow—and they continue to be vibrant today.

Similar roles were played by organizations such as the Improved Benevolent and Protective Order of Elks of the World, the Order of the Eastern Star, and Black mutual benefit societies that pooled resources to provide burial insurance, education funds, and care for widows and orphans.

These types of cultural support have been essential in preserving identity and belonging under ongoing conditions designed to force assimilation and fracture. Black fatigue intensifies when belonging is eroded or replaced with conditional acceptance. Healing, therefore, requires not only individual self-care but collective care. African-centered psychology makes clear that restoration is relational.

Pilgramages to Africa also restore a sense of belonging: Diasporans are often greeted upon landing with "welcome home."

When identity and belonging are grounded in the communal and relational principles of African-centered psychology, the question shifts from "Who do I have to be to belong?" to "Where do I inherently belong?" That shift is critical to healing Black fatigue.

REFLECTION

- Where in your life have you felt most like yourself, without effort?
- What would it be like if you stopped trying to belong in spaces where belonging has to be created and focused your energy on those spaces where your belonging is assumed and affirmed?
- Who has affirmed your identity without requiring explanation?
- What forms of belonging have sustained you, even quietly?
- Where might you be carrying more alone than you need to?

Summary

The Eurocentric, Western view of self is very different from the African-centered view, which prioritizes extended family, relationships, and communal practices. Within the Eurocentric model, responsibility, achievement, and failure are understood primarily as individual matters. The focus is on the individual and the nuclear family, with extended family considered secondary to success and survival. African-centered psychology, on the other hand, views identity and survival as collective, with well-being depending on shared responsibility and care.

These differences are especially evident in how belonging is understood. In Eurocentric frameworks, belonging is often conditional, something to be created, granted, or earned. In African-centered and Indigenous belief systems, belonging is inherent, assumed, and a birthright. It is not conferred by institutions or approval; it is rooted in kinship, history, and shared humanity.

Living in spaces where dominant values are assumed to be superior or the only way delegitimizes African and Indigenous ways of knowing and being. This persistent devaluation exacerbates Black fatigue.

Healing that fatigue requires returning to ourselves, reclaiming the right to self-identification by rejecting imposed identities and restoring ancestral and African-centered practices of healing and wellness. We explore these practices further in Parts II and III.

Part II

RECLAIMING POWER, AGENCY, AND VOICE

Power doesn't have to show off.
Power is confident, self-assuring, self-starting and self-stopping, self-warming and self-justifying.
When you have it, you know it.

—Ralph Ellison, American author, literary critic, and scholar[1]

FOUR

REMEMBERING, RECLAIMING, AND RESTORING THE VILLAGE

We are each other's harvest: we are each other's business: we are each other's magnitude and bond.

—Gwendolyn Brooks, poet, author, and teacher[2]

In Chapter 3, we described the essential role of community in creating a sense of belonging to support healing Black fatigue. In many African and Indigenous traditions, community is often understood as a "village"—a network of relationships grounded in shared responsibility and care. Historically and contemporarily, mutual aid networks, faith communities, and extended family have all functioned as villages, collectively affirming identity through relationships. In this way, the village remains a living, adaptive practice rather than a relic of the past.

This chapter traces a journey: remembering what the village originally provided, reclaiming its wisdom as legitimate and necessary to heal Black fatigue, and restoring its practices in ways that meet today's realities.

Why the Village Matters

We have all heard the phrase "It takes a village." The saying originated from the Nigerian Igbo proverb *Oran a azu nwa*, which loosely translates to "it takes the community/village to raise a child." Proverbs in other African cultures, such as the Swahili "One hand does not nurse a child," the Sudanese "A child is a child of everyone," and the Tanzanian "One knee does not bring up a child," convey the same sentiment.[3]

The phrase is widely recognized as having been popularized in the United States by Hillary Clinton, who used it as the title of her bestselling book and in her speech at the 1996 Democratic National Convention.[4] The reaction was largely split along political lines, with Democrats tending to welcome the message as a call for shared responsibility and communal support while Republicans framed it as an attack on parental autonomy, criticizing the notion as government overreach into private family life.

Bob Dole, then the Republican nominee for president, explicitly countered that it takes a *family*, not a village, to raise children. Some conservative commentators even ridiculed the expression, associating it with tribalism. This reception highlighted a continuing deep divide between African-centered communalism and Western individualism, as discussed in Chapters 2 and 3.

In African worldviews, the village is a living social system whose role extends beyond child rearing. Before colonization, enslavement, and the global spread of individualism, African societies generally organized life around communal responsibility, shared identity, and collective survival. The erosion of village structures did not occur because they were ineffective or inferior; they were intentionally disrupted and delegitimized. The consequences of that disruption, including social fragmentation, isolation, and overburdened individuals, have greatly contributed to Black fatigue.

Healing Black fatigue requires more than individual coping strategies. It requires remembering what was whole, reclaiming what was mischaracterized as deficient, and restoring what was taken through violence, displacement, and imposed cultural norms.

In her book *The Cost of Healing in Silence: Navigating Racial Trauma and the Call for Culturally Responsive Care*, Ashley McGirt-Adair asserts that healing does not occur in isolation, nor can it be divorced from identity, history, and community.[5] When healing ignores culture, individuals often feel that they must suffer in silence, carrying pain privately in systems that neither see nor affirm their lived realities. This is the opposite of what is experienced in village structures, where collective sharing of pain and other burdens makes the load a little bit lighter.

Remembering the Village: A West African Example

Let's remember a specific example of an African village. One illustrative example is the Yoruba culture in southwestern Nigeria, although similar structures existed across West Africa.[6]

Traditional Yoruba villages were organized around extended family compounds (*agbo ile*), where multiple generations lived together or in close proximity. These compounds were centers of socialization, caregiving, economic cooperation, spiritual practice, and governance. Children were raised collectively. Elders held authority not because of wealth or dominance, but because of wisdom and a shared sense of responsibility to the community.

Leadership was distributed across roles, including chiefs, councils of elders, women's collectives, and spiritual leaders, creating systems of accountability and balance. No single individual was expected to meet all of their needs alone. When hardship occurred, such as illness, death, or financial strain, the burden was absorbed by the community.

Spirit and daily life were inseparable. Rituals, storytelling, festivals, and ancestral remembrance reinforced shared identity and continuity across generations. In this context, belonging was assumed. One did not need to earn community; one was born into it.

While modern political and economic forces have transformed many rural communities and urban migration has changed how extended families co-reside, the idea of the village remains embedded in Yoruba culture today.

Our Villages

Mary-Frances remembers:

Growing up in Niagara Falls, New York, I lived on a street made up almost entirely of Black families. I emphasize street because the surrounding blocks were predominantly white. Our street was its own ecosystem, a small, close-knit village.

I remember Ms. Alita (not her real name), who "mothered" every child in the neighborhood. She kept a vigilant eye on us as we walked home from school, quick to correct our behavior or call our parents if we stepped out of line. In fact, by the time I reached my own house just six doors down, she had often already phoned my mother with a full report of any mischief. As a child, I found her constant watchfulness annoying, even unfair. I wanted her to mind her own business!

But now I understand: She was the village in action. Her vigilance was not nosiness; it was care. It was protection. It was community responsibility made visible.

Mareisha recalls:

I remember the village that the Perinton African American Heritage Committee, which we described in the Chapter 3, created for me. Living in a predominantly white suburb could easily have left me feeling isolated or unseen. But instead of loneliness, I experienced belonging. I had an extended family—"aunties," and friends who felt like sisters, brothers, and cousins—who looked out for me, guided me, and made sure I never felt alone in spaces where I might have otherwise been the only Black child.

Just as my mother experienced in her own childhood village, the "aunties" in my life were not always subtle in their interventions. Their correction was not always welcomed in the moment—but now, as an adult, I deeply appreciate what their presence meant.

The village continues to live across generations and geographies, carried forward not only through memory, but through everyday acts of care. These enduring patterns of connection and collective responsibility continue to shape how many people of African descent understand self, belonging, and community today.

One of Mary-Frances's Barbadian acquaintances recently shared a story that beautifully illustrates this continuity. In his neighborhood, people regularly gather to cook together on an outdoor grill and stove. No single person provides everything. One brings rice, another freshly caught fish, another breadfruit picked from trees growing in nearby yards. Each offering reflects what that person or family can contribute. For elders and neighbors who are homebound, meals are delivered directly to their doors. He explained that while members of the community do not have much by conventional measures, sharing has always been their way of living—an intergenerational practice rooted in care, reciprocity, and a deep understanding and appreciation for the village.

REFLECTION

- What stories, memories, or practices from your family or community reflect collective care, shared responsibility, or extended kinship?
- How were elders, children, and those in need supported in your family or community when you were growing up?
- In what ways have you seen African or diasporic village practices continue informally or quietly in your own life?
- What has been lost, disrupted, or forgotten about communal life because of migration, assimilation, or survival pressures?
- How does remembering these structures challenge narratives that frame Black communal life as deficient or dysfunctional?

Reclaiming and Restoring the Village

Reclaiming the village begins with rejecting the idea that African and Indigenous communal practices are somehow backward, inefficient, or incompatible with modern life. As we discussed in Chapter 3, these judgments emerge from Eurocentric frameworks that privilege independence, competition, and nuclear family structures as universal ideals.

African-centered psychology reminds us that interdependence is a fundamental principle that is essential to reclaiming who we are as communal, relational beings. Wade W. Nobles and other African-centered scholars emphasize that wellness is measured not by autonomy, but by harmony, balance, and right relationship with others and the environment.

Reclaiming the village requires naming communal ways of being as legitimate sources of strength. This includes reclaiming:

- Extended family and "chosen" kin as real family
- Collective caregiving as a responsibility, not a burden
- Shared resources as strategic, not dependent
- Spiritual and ritual practices as healing, not fantasy or superstition

When these practices are dismissed or pathologized, Black people are forced into making decisions that may not feel right for us—but the pressure and entrenchment of dominant ways make it difficult, and sometimes impossible, to resist them.

Healing Practices for Reclaiming the Village

Reclaiming the village might start with:

- *Faith and spiritual communities* that function as extended family, offering emotional, material, and spiritual support
- *Healing circles* and support groups grounded in shared identity rather than individual diagnosis
- *Rituals of remembrance*, such as libations, ancestor acknowledgment, and storytelling
- *Naming and renaming practices* that restore identity and lineage

These practices reconnect individuals to collective meaning, reducing the burden of carrying pain alone. As Ashley McGirt-Adair said in an interview about her book *The Cost of Healing in Silence*, "Healing does not only happen in therapy offices. Peer support, healing circles, cultural practices, and community-led interventions must be funded, legitimized, and integrated into the mental health ecosystem, not treated as fringe or supplemental options."[7] See Chapter 9 for a step-by-step process to create a micro-village healing circle.

REFLECTION

- Which communal practices in your life have you minimized, hidden, or felt pressured to justify?
- How might naming African and Indigenous ways of being as legitimate shift how you view your own needs for support and connection?
- What healing practices—spiritual, cultural, relational—have helped you feel more grounded or whole?
- What would it mean for you to reclaim interdependence as a strength rather than a liability?

Restoring the Village: Learning from Global Communal Models

Restoration asks a harder question: How do we rebuild what was intentionally taken from us?

Many immigrant communities arriving in the United States bring communal economic models with them. In some East and Southeast Asian communities, for example, rotating savings and credit associations (often called *hui*, *tandas*, or *chit funds*) pool resources so one member can start a business, buy a home, or stabilize their family. Once established, that person contributes to the next member's success. These systems are built on trust, reciprocity, and collective advancement.

As mentioned in Chapter 3, Black communities in the United States have historically practiced similar models, in the form of mutual aid societies, fraternal organizations, churches, cooperatives, and freedom schools. Many of these structures remain in place today, but while some continue to thrive, others have been weakened by discriminatory policies and practices such as redlining and predatory lending, as well as internalized narratives that equate success with individualism rather than collectivism.

Why Restoration Is Hard—and Necessary

Restoring the village today is challenging because it requires going against dominant values that have repeatedly betrayed, delegitimized, and even banned Black communal efforts. It is hard and fatiguing to buck systems that promote individualism through practice, policy, and legislation.

Coexisting in a society where Western, Eurocentric ways are considered the only accepted norm requires creativity, tenacity, and some adaptation. Restoration does not mean recreating the past exactly as it was; it means authentically adapting village principles to present realities. This can take many forms, including:

REBUILDING INTERGENERATIONAL CONNECTIONS

- Create intentional spaces where elders, adults, youth, and children interact regularly, not just in moments of crisis, but as a way of life. Barbershops are a prime example of the village in practice. For generations, these spaces have offered far more than haircuts. They have functioned as cultural hubs—places where Black men of all ages can gather outside the white gaze, speak freely, and be wholly themselves, sharing stories, debating current events, teaching life lessons, and seeking advice without judgment. In many ways, the barbershop operates as an informal therapeutic space.
- Restore the role of elders as knowledge keepers, mentors, and moral anchors.
- Encourage youth to contribute as teachers, especially in digital literacy, social media, and contemporary cultural expression. As

a real-life example, Teens Teach Tech is a program that empowers young people to lead digital literacy workshops in their own communities.[8] Similarly, The Hidden Genius Project trains Black male high school students as youth educators, teaching coding and computer skills to younger students of color.[9] Even outside these formal programs, research shows that Black girls and other youth often serve as the most digitally fluent members of their families, guiding siblings, parents, and elders in navigating online spaces.[10] In these ways, they are restoring the intergenerational exchange of knowledge that has always been central to the village.

PRACTICING COMMUNAL CARE INSTEAD OF INDIVIDUAL SURVIVALISM

- Shift from "I have to do it all" to "We hold each other up," through mutual aid networks, shared childcare circles, community gardening, and similar initiatives.
- Normalize asking for help; recognize that seeking support is a reflection of cultural strength, not personal failure.
- Build micro-villages within workplaces, faith communities, neighborhoods, and friend groups. The employee resource groups that have gained popularity in corporate spaces can serve as micro-villages; however, they are usually structured with rules and requirements that may inhibit communal care. Also, some dominant group members see these groups as divisive, another factor that exacerbates Black fatigue.

DESIGNING CULTURALLY ROOTED HEALING SPACES

- Organize healing circles, storysharing gatherings, and communal rituals grounded in African diasporic traditions.
- Reclaim practices such as libation ceremonies, communal meals, drumming, movement, and meditation as methods for collective restoration.
- Bring joy, creativity, and cultural expression into healing (because Black joy is itself a communal act of resistance).

PROTECTING TIME, SPACE, AND ENERGY FROM WESTERN NORMS

- Push back against urgency, overwork, and perfectionism—traits of Western individualism—by setting boundaries and adopting community-centered rhythms.
- Design schedules, workflows, and organizational cultures that allow for rest, reflection, and relational time.
- Encourage "village sabbaths" or collective rest days, whether in families, workplaces, or community groups. The Winters Group adopted a practice of "wellness" days for team members that were separate from sick leave.

REVIVING COLLECTIVE ACCOUNTABILITY AND SHARED WISDOM

- Return to the principle that everyone is responsible for everyone else's well-being as a shared ethic.
- Encourage bystander care: checking on neighbors, intervening when someone is harmed, celebrating each other's wins.
- Create shared agreements for how communities communicate, resolve conflict, and support those dealing with racial trauma.

REIMAGINING THE VILLAGE THROUGH TECHNOLOGY

- Use digital platforms to maintain community: virtual check-ins, group chats, online mentoring circles, and teletherapy groups.
- Create private online "villages" where Black people can gather without surveillance, judgment, or cultural misunderstanding. Mary-Frances is a member of several online villages where sharing is open, unfiltered, and affirming. It brings joy and alleviates Black fatigue.
- Revive the call-and-response tradition digitally, amplifying voices, stories, and urgent needs across platforms.

BUILDING NEW COMMUNAL ECONOMIES

- Support Black-owned businesses, cooperatives, and collectives.
- Establish community investment circles, savings clubs, and skill-sharing networks.
- Shift from competitive individual gain to shared economic uplift.

RESTORING COMMUNAL APPROACHES TO RAISING CHILDREN

- Have "aunties," "uncles," godparents, and trusted neighbors actively participate in children's lives.
- Create community tutoring groups, youth leadership programs, and safe intergenerational play spaces.
- Recognize that every child in the community is "our child" and worthy of protection, guidance, and opportunity.

STRENGTHENING EMOTIONAL AND PSYCHOLOGICAL SAFETY

- Build relational ecosystems where Black people can unmask, exhale, and be fully human, such as the "Sista Friends" group described in Chapter 3.
- Offer trauma-informed community support grounded in affirmation, not judgment.
- Cultivate environments where vulnerability is welcomed and met with compassion rather than critique.

RECLAIMING COLLECTIVE PURPOSE

- Restore the belief that community itself is the best source of power.
- Create shared missions centered on advocacy, justice, learning, spiritual growth, and cultural preservation.
- Reconnect to the ancestral understanding that the village exists because we need each other to survive.

Summary

Sociopolitical polarization, anti-Black racism, and dehumanization of those who are outside the dominant culture continue to intensify. Black fatigue is reaching unprecedented levels. Remembering the original meaning of the village, reclaiming its wisdom, and restoring its practices are acts of healing, resistance, survival, and joy. Remembering allows us to see what was whole. Reclaiming allows us to name it as valid. Restoring allows us to practice it again, imperfectly, intentionally, and together.

FIVE
RESISTANCE AS HEALING

Revolution begins with the self, in the self.

—Toni Cade Bambara, writer, filmmaker, and social activist[1]

To understand resistance as healing, we must recognize it not only as opposition to injustice but as a spiritual, embodied, cognitive, and communal practice. In the same way the village sustains belonging (see Chapter 4), resistance sustains dignity. This chapter explores how resistance has functioned across generations as a means of protecting humanity, restoring balance, and healing Black fatigue.

The Deep Roots of Resistance as Sacred Protection

The broader understanding of resistance has deep roots. To fully understand resistance as a form of healing, it helps to look back at how Black resistance has manifested across generations. From African societies to the African diaspora in the Americas, Black communities have developed ways to protect dignity, preserve community, and sustain life in the face of disruption and injustice. The principle of *Sankofa*, which reminds us to look to the past in order to build a better future, invites us to revisit these histories and consider how traditions of resistance continue to inform how we respond to harm today.

African-Centered Foundations: Protection of Land, Spirit, and Community

In African history, resistance has long functioned as a means of protecting land, spirit, and community. Warrior traditions, for example, organized systems of defense responsible for protecting villages, safeguarding territory, and maintaining social stability. Their role extended beyond warfare; those entrusted with defense were also expected to uphold shared values and act when leadership threatened the well-being of the people.

Women played critical roles in resistance and protection as well. Leaders such as Queen Nzinga of Ndongo and Matamba in 17th-century Angola used diplomacy, alliance building, and military strategy to challenge Portuguese colonization.[2] In West Africa, Yaa Asantewaa, queen mother of the Asante, led a war of independence that came to be known as the War of the Golden Stool against British colonial forces in 1900, when the kingdom's spiritual authority was threatened.[3]

Spiritual insight was equally central to resistance during this time. Foretelling, ritual practice, and ancestral guidance were often relied upon to inform decisions about conflict, negotiation, and protection. Spiritual leaders helped communities interpret threats, maintain connections with ancestors, and restore balance when social harmony was disrupted.

These traditions traveled with Africans across the Atlantic, shaping the ways enslaved people resisted, preserved their humanity, and sustained community under conditions of extreme oppression.

Resistance During Enslavement: Preservation of Humanity

As discussed in previous chapters, the trafficking of enslaved Africans and the system of chattel slavery were designed not only to extract labor but to strip away identity, autonomy, and belonging. Enslaved Africans were legally defined as property, separated from family and community ties, denied legal personhood, and subjected to constant surveillance and violence.

The institution of slavery sought to suppress cultural memory and to control spiritual practices and beliefs. It isolated individuals from one another and from the traditions that anchored their identities and ways of life. And through it all, enslaved people found ways to resist.

Some acts of resistance were more visible and confrontational, such as revolts, rebellions, and attempts at escape that directly challenged the authority of enslavers. Enslaved people who fled plantations formed what were known as "maroon communities"—independent communities established by formerly enslaved people throughout the Americas, particularly in the Caribbean and Brazil.[4]

One of the most well-known leaders of the maroons in Jamaica was Nanny of the Maroons, an 18th-century spiritual and military leader who helped organize resistance against British colonial forces.[5] Drawing on African spiritual traditions and knowledge of the mountainous landscape, Nanny helped lead guerrilla campaigns to protect maroon communities and preserve their autonomy.

Resistance during this time was expressed through everyday, subtle acts too. Historians have documented resistance tactics such as work slowdowns, tool-breaking, feigned illness, secret literacy, and efforts to maintain family and community ties despite forced separation. Oral histories and cultural accounts also describe practices such as enslaved people laughing into barrels or other enclosed spaces so the sound would not carry to enslavers.[6] In this way, laughter itself became an act of resistance (we talk more about joy as a form of resistance later in this chapter).

Spiritual life was central to the preservation of humanity and dignity. Enslaved people gathered in hush harbors—secret religious meetings held in wooded areas beyond the direct gaze and control of the enslavers—to pray, sing, and interpret scripture through their own lived experience.[7] In these spaces, worship was a source of strength and connection. Spiritual life also included communal rituals that helped sustain cultural memory and belonging. For example, the ring shout, a sacred ritual rooted in West African traditions, allowed enslaved Africans from different ethnic groups to preserve spiritual traditions and connect through shared movement and rhythm, even when they did not share a common language.[8] Conjure work or rootwork (Hoodoo) also emerged from Central and West African traditions, incorporating Indigenous American botanical knowledge and Christian elements. It was used for healing, protection, and at times to guard against violence or mistreatment.

Music was one of the most powerful forms of resistance available to enslaved people. Spirituals and work songs expressed faith, sorrow, and hope. Often referred to as "sorrow songs," they reflected the power of naming one's pain while refusing to be defined by it and provided sources of healing and uplift.[9]

They also served as warnings and teaching tools. For example, the well-known spiritual "Wade in the Water" has long been understood within Black oral tradition as providing instruction alongside its spiritual message.[10] The refrain urging listeners to "wade in the water" has been interpreted as an instruction to get into the water to evade being detected by dogs used to hunt those seeking freedom. Some accounts suggest that abolitionist Harriet Tubman used the song as part of her escape strategies. Whether sung in the fields or in hidden gatherings, sorrow songs connected worship, survival, and resistance. In later generations, music would become a staple of the civil rights movement, carrying forward this legacy of resistance.

Resistance during enslavement protected identity, faith, shared knowledge, and dignity.

Post-Emancipation Resistance

As highlighted in Chapter 3, although formal enslavement was largely abolished by the mid-19th century, racial terror, economic exclusion, segregation, and disenfranchisement continued, contributing further to Black fatigue. Black communities continued to navigate systems that limited opportunity, restricted mobility, and made it necessary to constantly adapt. During this time, resistance remained essential, not only as opposition but also as a way to heal Black fatigue through collective organization, shared resources, and communal care.

MUTUAL AID SOCIETIES

As noted in Chapter 3, mutual aid societies had already emerged among free Black communities before emancipation and expanded significantly afterward.[11] These organizations served as collective systems of care, providing burial insurance, financial assistance, medical support, and educational resources at a time when public institutions either excluded Black families or actively undermined their well-being.

In the United States, organizations such as the Grand United Order of True Reformers and Prince Hall Masonic lodges offered financial support, insurance programs, and leadership infrastructure within Black communities. Many also became cultural and community centers and were closely connected to Black churches. In the Caribbean, similar systems of collective care developed through organizations known as "friendly societies," which operated much like mutual aid societies in the United States.[12]

Mutual aid was not simply charity but a shared commitment to survival. Members paid into a common fund, pooling limited resources so care could be distributed collectively. These societies reduced isolation and helped stabilize families navigating constant insecurity. They functioned as a way of addressing Black fatigue by ensuring that the burden of survival was not carried individually.

ORGANIZED RESISTANCE

Organized resistance during the Jim Crow era in the United States extended the tradition of collective action. Boycotts, legal challenges, voter registration efforts, and mass mobilizations were strategies used to confront systemic injustice and reduce the cumulative strain placed on Black communities. Supported by churches, civic organizations, and mutual aid societies, these movements drew on the same traditions of care and responsibility that have long sustained the village. They sought not only legal change but also the restoration of dignity, safety, and access.

REFLECTION

Resistance is often framed as disruption. Yet many of the examples we have explored so far show resistance functioning as protection, restoration, and communal care. Consider:

- What forms of resistance might you have inherited from your ancestors?
- Where have you seen resistance operate as protection or care, either in your own life or within your community?

Present-Day Resistance as Healing

In today's society, Black people who name racial harm or question unfairness are frequently labeled as overly sensitive, difficult, or divisive. Resistance is often treated by the dominant culture as inherently disruptive, equated with anger, defiance, and unlawfulness. But as we have explored in this chapter, African traditions of resistance have long been understood as necessary for preserving dignity and collective well-being.

Black fatigue deepens when we live too long without resisting systems that were built to dehumanize us. When we are expected to adapt, overperform, and shrink ourselves in service of white supremacist norms, the exhaustion accumulates.

In the context of healing Black fatigue, resistance is about setting limits, naming harm, and refusing misalignment. It is how we restore balance (Ma'at), illuminate the spirit (Sakhu), and protect our sense of wholeness.

William Cross's Nigrescence model, discussed in Chapter 1, reminds us that identity development often involves rejecting imposed narratives. Resistance is central to that process. When we refuse deficit-based definitions or challenge distorted portrayals of Blackness, we are actively shaping a healed, self-defined Black identity.

Resistance appears in the everyday choices we make to protect our dignity, preserve our energy, and remain aligned with our values. These practices may not look dramatic, but they play an important role in healing Black fatigue by interrupting the constant demands placed on Black bodies, minds, and spirits.

Rest as Protection

In her 1988 book *A Burst of Light*, writer and activist Audre Lorde wrote that caring for herself was not self-indulgence but self-preservation.[13] Lorde reminds us that protecting one's energy has long been connected to survival in systems that disregard Black humanity.

In recent years, Tricia Hersey, founder of The Nap Ministry, has helped popularize the idea that rest itself can be a form of resistance, challenging the cultural narrative that equates productivity with worth.[14] Choosing rest over constant output pushes back on the sense of urgency and counters the pressure to constantly prove value through performance.

Of course, rest alone does not eliminate the racist structures that contribute to Black fatigue. However, it can restore the energy needed to navigate and confront them. Rest helps clear the mind and strengthen the body, thereby functioning as a form of both protection and preparation.

In Chapter 8, we offer a rest practice that can support in healing Black fatigue.

Saying No: Boundary Setting

Boundaries safeguard one's time and energy. In environments where a sense of urgency is normalized and overperformance is expected, the absence of boundaries can quietly erode well-being and exacerbate Black fatigue. Choosing not to accept every request, shoulder every burden, or engage in every debate reduces the slow erosion that occurs when energy is continuously depleted without being restored.

Boundary setting doesn't have to be confrontational, and you do not need to feel guilty about setting limits on your time. It also does not require lengthy explanations or justifications. Here are a few examples of boundary statements:

"I'm not able to take that on right now."

"I need some time to think about that before I commit."

"This conversation isn't something I'm willing to engage in today."

"I am not comfortable speaking on behalf of all Black people."

"I can help with this piece, but I cannot take responsibility for the whole thing."

"I'm not comfortable with that."

"I am choosing to rest today."

Within an African-centered framework, boundary setting reflects a commitment to Ma'at. It helps to restore balance when demands undermine one's dignity, capacity, and energy. Saying no becomes an act of alignment rather than selfishness or hostility, and a way of protecting one's mental and physical health and sense of self-worth.

See Chapter 6 for more suggestions on setting boundaries, specifically in the workplace.

Black Joy as Renewal

Practicing joy in environments where racialized harm is persistent and where dominant narratives about Black life often emphasize struggle, trauma, or oppression interrupts the assumption that suffering must be the storyline. It creates space for breath, laughter, creativity, and connection.

The goal of joy as a tool of resistance is not to deny the existence of injustice, but to allow joy to coexist alongside it and affirm that Black life is not solely defined by suffering. Joy helps renew the spirit and replenish the energy needed to keep resisting. It strengthens our capacity to continue naming harm, setting boundaries, and seeking alignment without becoming consumed by Black fatigue. Practiced intentionally, joy can be both a refuge and a resource.

In Chapter 8, we explore small practices of joy that can be incorporated into everyday life to support healing from Black fatigue.

Protecting Your Spirit from the White Gaze

W. E. B. Du Bois described the weight of seeing oneself through the eyes of society that devalues Blackness as "double-consciousness."[15] Decades later, author Toni Morrison expanded this conversation through what she called the white gaze, naming the pressure to center white perspectives, validation, or understanding. This is a familiar experience for many Black people who navigate predominantly white spaces.

The constant code switching, emotional regulation, and feeling of needing to always remain on guard demand significant mental and emotional effort. Over time, that effort wears a person down and contributes to Black fatigue.

Healing Black fatigue in these moments might look like speaking without excessive disclaimers, resisting the urge to constantly translate one's experience for others, or allowing one's tone, language, and presence to exist without adjustment for another's comfort. Protecting your spirit from the white gaze does not mean ignoring the realities of the spaces you are in. It means recognizing when the pressure to explain or adjust yourself is draining and, when possible, allowing yourself to let that pressure go.

Speaking Truth Without Minimizing

Resistance today can also appear as naming harm clearly rather than minimizing it. In many environments, as a survival strategy, Black people have learned to soften their language, downplay their experiences, or frame concerns in ways that feel less threatening to others. For example, someone may feel it's easier to describe a racist comment as "probably just a misunderstanding," even when it clearly caused harm. Speaking truth without minimizing harm might instead sound like, "That comment was hurtful, and I want to explain why." Or you may choose to leave it at "That comment was hurtful," if you do not have the energy or capacity to explain further.

Of course, naming harm clearly can be easier said than done. In environments where psychological safety is limited or nonexistent, you have to consider the risks of speaking up, and how you choose to do so. Protecting your well-being sometimes means using a different strategy.

While speaking your truth without minimizing may not always produce immediate change, it can protect your sense of integrity and self-respect, both of which are essential for healing Black fatigue.

Refusing Deficit-Based Narratives

For generations, Black life has often been framed through assumptions of deficiency, dysfunction, or failure. These narratives have been used to justify inequitable systems and to distort how Black identity is understood. Over time, this messaging can become internalized, influencing how Black people see themselves and their communities. Holding onto these distorted narratives contributes to the emotional and psychological toll that fuels Black fatigue and erodes dignity and humanity.

Refusing those narratives is a commitment to a fuller and more accurate understanding of Black life—one that recognizes resilience, creativity, intellect, and communal strength. When Black people resist internalizing deficit-based assumptions, they protect how Black identity is defined and understood. Developing a grounded Black identity often requires reframing the narratives that have been imposed on us and reclaiming the right to define ourselves. Cross's Nigrescence model describes this process as a central part of Black identity development.

In Chapter 8, we share a healing practice to reframe deficit-based narratives.

REFLECTION

Many forms of resistance are subtle and personal. They may appear as boundaries, truth-telling, rest, or moments of joy. Consider:

- What actions in your life might actually be forms of resistance protecting your dignity, energy, or identity?
- What have you been taught is "too much," "too angry," or "unprofessional" that may actually be a form of resistance protecting your spirit or preserving your well-being?

Summary

Resistance is often thought of as an act of disruption or defiance. Yet across African traditions and throughout the African diaspora, resistance has consistently functioned as a means of protecting and preserving dignity, identity, and community life. From the spiritual practices of enslaved Africans to the mutual aid networks that sustained families after emancipation and the everyday acts of boundary setting and truth-telling today, resistance has helped safeguard humanity in systems that frequently deny it.

Healing Black fatigue does not always begin with large-scale change. When individuals reclaim their right to rest, speak truth, and refuse harmful narratives, they continue a long tradition of resistance that sustains both personal and collective well-being.

SIX

NAVIGATING THE WORKPLACE

If you lie to yourself about your own pain, you will be killed by those who will claim you enjoyed it.

—Alice Walker, author and social activist[1]

For many Black people, the workplace is a space where identity, dignity, and spirit are constantly negotiated. As we discuss in our book *Black Fatigue*, the exhaustion of navigating ~~micro~~aggressions, the pressure to constantly prove one's competence, and the emotional labor required to function within systems that were not designed with us in mind results in fatigue that manifests in visible and invisible ways.

We both shared stories about our workplace experiences in the Introduction. Many Black people who we know personally or professionally or who have been participants in our sessions at The Winters Group have shared similar stories about feeling unseen, being held to unequal standards, or having their competence questioned despite their qualifications and contributions. They describe the constant calculation of deciding how they should show up at work, when to speak up, and how much of their authentic selves they feel safe bringing into professional spaces.

In the Western world, in particular, workplaces are built on values that often conflict with African-centered understandings of self and community. Professional environments tend to prioritize individualism, hierarchy, competition, and productivity. Success, for example, is frequently measured through individual performance metrics. Consider the performance review: Even though we may work in team environments, we are still evaluated on our individual contributions. Success in this way becomes something to compete for rather than something that is shared collectively.

As discussed in Chapters 2 and 3, African-centered psychology understands the self as relational—connected to family, community, ancestry, and spiritual purpose. For Black people, the tension between these worldviews is often compounded by racialized expectations such as heightened scrutiny, pressure to code-switch, and subtle messages that one must continually prove one's worth.

In this chapter, our focus is not on revisiting the harm—something we explored extensively in *Black Fatigue*—but on restoration. We explore ways Black employees can reclaim agency, protect their spirits, and navigate workplace environments to minimize Black fatigue and support healing.

Work Within the Black Historical Context

The fatigue many Black people experience in today's workplace has roots in enslavement, which fundamentally reshaped the relationship between Black people and work. It is rooted in centuries of racialized systems that extracted value from the work of Black people while denying their humanity. Understanding this history helps explain why the modern workplace can feel so misaligned with our well-being. It also reminds us that the relationship between Black people and work has not always looked the way it does today.

Labor Under Enslavement

When Africans were forcibly taken from their homelands and transported to the Americas, including the Caribbean, the meaning of work changed. What had once been connected to community, land, and collective survival was transformed into forced labor under systems built on domination and control.

During enslavement, the work of Black people was violently controlled and constantly surveilled. Enslaved people had no ownership over their work, their bodies, or the fruits of their labor. Every aspect of daily life was monitored—the pace of work, the output, obedience, behavior. This unrelenting oversight enforced compliance and reinforced a racial hierarchy that treated Black people as property rather than human beings. The result was a profound disruption of identity, reducing Black people to the labor they could produce and redefining human worth through productivity rather than community, lineage, or spiritual purpose.

Post-Emancipation Labor Systems

After emancipation, new systems emerged that continued to extract value from Black labor while limiting opportunity. Sharecropping, domestic work, and convict leasing tied many Black workers to exploitative economic conditions. Although the legal institution of slavery had ended, the underlying dynamics of control and extraction persisted. Scholars of racial capitalism have shown how Black labor continued to fuel economic systems while Black humanity remained marginalized.[2]

One egregious example of how exploitation persisted after emancipation is the convict leasing system in states such as Alabama in the late 19th and early 20th centuries.[3] After the Civil War, many Southern states passed so-called Black Codes that criminalized everyday activities for newly freed Black people, such as vagrancy, loitering, changing employers without permission, or even "insulting gestures." Once arrested under these discriminatory laws, Black people—overwhelmingly Black men—were convicted through biased local courts and then leased to private companies for labor. Companies paid the state, not the workers, creating a profit incentive for mass arrests. Conditions were extremely dangerous. In Alabama coal mines, operated by companies such as US Steel, death rates for leased convicts were extraordinarily high.

Modern Workplaces

While today's workplaces look very different from these earlier systems, some of the same patterns remain.

Surveillance has taken on new forms: productivity metrics, performance dashboards, behavioral evaluations, tone policing. Research shows that Black employees are often evaluated more harshly than their peers and are more likely to receive vague or personality-based criticism rather than actionable feedback tied to advancement.

For example, Textio, an augmented writing platform, surveyed over twenty-five thousand business employees and analyzed performance feedback documents. The study revealed consistent patterns of inequity by gender, race, and age. Latinx and Black employees were 2.4 times more likely to receive job performance feedback that was negatively biased (e.g., based on personality traits rather than job duties) and not actionable.[4]

According to research published in *The Economic Journal*, Black employees are also more heavily monitored than white workers in their first year of employment.[5] As a result, they're more likely to be let go than non-Black workers before one year of seniority. The study's coauthor, Costas Cavounidis, summarized the results as follows: "If you're a white worker, it's pretty easy to stay employed if you're not that good, whereas if you're Black, you will be monitored. And if you're not that capable, you will be fired at a higher rate than a similarly skilled white worker. . . . White workers can skate by in this sense."[6]

Many Black employees find themselves as the only one, or one of a few, of their race in an organization, on a team, in a meeting, or within leadership. This experience, often described as *tokenism*, can produce a paradox in which Black people feel both hypervisible and invisible at the same time. Mistakes may be magnified while contributions are overlooked. Black employees may serve as visible symbols of diversity while remaining excluded from decision-making power.

Understanding this historical continuity reminds us that the tension many Black people experience at work today is not simply individual burnout. It reflects a longer history of racialized labor systems that continue to shape modern workplace dynamics and influence how identity and worth are interpreted. The question then becomes: How do we navigate these environments without losing our sense of self?

Reclaiming Your Worth Beyond the Workplace

Western culture places professional identity at the center of self-worth. Many people are taught, explicitly or implicitly, that their value is determined by their career. When you meet someone new, how often is "What do you do?" one of the first questions asked?

The Extended Self

In Part I, we introduced the concept of the extended self. In African-centered psychology, as discussed in Chapters 2 and 3, identity extends beyond the individual to include family, community, ancestors, culture, and spiritual purpose.

In this worldview, the spirit (Sakhu) holds deeper significance than job titles or professional accolades. Ethical alignment with Ma'at—the principles of balance, justice, and truth—is valued more than status or advancement.

This understanding can be profoundly grounding for those navigating racialized workplaces. When work is no longer the center of your identity, workplace judgments cannot define the totality of who you are or your inherent worth.

Rejecting Workplace Narratives

Many workplace narratives send subtle messages that Black employees don't really belong, as we discussed in Chapter 3. These narratives may appear in coded feedback like:

- "You're not a cultural fit."
- "You need to work on your communication style."
- "You're not quite ready for leadership."
- "You're very passionate."

These phrases often reflect unspoken expectations about who is seen as professional, competent, or leadership material. As mentioned earlier, they often also are not related to the person's work and not actionable.

Part of healing Black fatigue and protecting our well-being is learning to recognize these narratives for what they are and refusing to internalize them as truths about our worth or capability. Rather than accepting them as accurate reflections of personal deficiencies, we can evaluate them within a broader understanding of how they are shaped by norms and biases that favor the dominant culture.

African-centered traditions remind us that identity and worth are not defined by external validation but by our connection to community, purpose, and spirit. When we view ourselves from this perspective, we can begin to reject workplace narratives that attempt to undermine who we are and what we are capable of. One way to resist these narratives is to consciously reframe them for yourself:

"You're not a cultural fit."	→	"The unique perspective that I bring can expand and strengthen the culture of this organization." (Their message suggests they do not value diversity.)
"You need to be more professional."	→	"Who defines professionalism? If their concept is misaligned with mine, it does not mean that I am not professional."
"You're not quite ready for leadership."	→	"Leadership can look different from the models this system has historically rewarded. My approach is equally valuable."

Central to this reframing is remembering that our value is not determined by how closely we conform to someone else's expectations. Our identities, experiences, and ways of showing up in the world are not deficits to be corrected; they speak to our uniqueness and the gifts we bring.

At the same time, growth and development remain important. Feedback can be evaluated through the lens of self-awareness, asking for specific examples that clarify the critique. It can be helpful to process such comments over time, and even to seek input from trusted friends and colleagues who will be honest with us. Taking a holistic and realistic approach allows us to reflect more thoughtfully and respond with intention.

REFLECTION

- When have you received feedback that was totally inconsistent with your own self-concept? What did you do about it?
- When have you received feedback that was surprising but, on reflection, you came to see was accurate? How did you act on it?
- When have you received feedback that you thought was racially biased? How did you respond?

Another common dynamic is the pressure to code-switch, adjusting language, tone, or behavior to conform to dominant cultural expectations. That pressure stems from the constant awareness of how one is perceived through the eyes of others. Code switching may be a choice we make in the moment to protect our peace, safety, or spirit—but that choice should remain ours.

Our colleagues, DEI practitioners and strategists Jerad Green and Andrea Pérez-Maikkula, offer the concept of "psychological agency" as a way of thinking about this dynamic.[7] Psychological agency reminds us that we have the power to decide how much of ourselves we bring into a space, when we do so, and with whom. Exercising this agency allows us to navigate workplaces with intention rather than feeling obligated to constantly reshape ourselves to fit expectations that were never designed with us in mind.

As we discuss in *Black Fatigue*, Black employees are also frequently expected to take on additional roles at work on top of their primary job responsibilities, such as educating colleagues about racism, mentoring other employees of color, or participating in DEI initiatives. This extra work is often not compensated and can take a psychological and physical toll. Naming these dynamics is an important step in rejecting them. We are not obligated to carry every burden placed upon us, nor to accept the expectation that we must give more of ourselves without recognition or compensation.

Layered onto these experiences is the persistent myth of meritocracy—the belief that success is determined purely by talent and hard work. In reality, access to opportunity is shaped by networks, bias, historical inequalities, and organizational structures that advantage some groups over others. Recognizing meritocracy as inherently subjective, with definitions of "merit" grounded in Western value systems that privilege dominant cultural norms while overlooking others, can help free us from accepting its measures as reflections of our personal worth.

Remember: Your value and dignity are not defined by the narratives your workplace attempts to impose. When we recognize and reject these narratives and form strong self-concepts grounded in African-centered psychology, we reclaim the authority to define our own worth.

Reclaiming Work

Reclaiming our relationship with work can help restore a sense of agency and bring our labor back into alignment with our values, purpose, and spirit.

Work does not have to define us. It can be understood as:

A CHOICE, NOT A DESTINY

Increasing numbers of Black people are exploring entrepreneurship and alternative career pathways that allow for greater control and autonomy over their labor and purpose. Black women start businesses at the highest rate of any demographic group in the United States, with 17 percent engaged in launching new ventures, compared with 10 percent of white women and 15 percent of white men.[8]

We both have experience with this. Mary-Frances left the corporate world after a short time to start her own business over forty years ago, and despite the uncertainty of whether that business would succeed, the lifting of the burden of being othered, minoritized, and not valued far outweighed that risk. Mareisha left the corporate world after eight years to join The Winters Group and felt an immediate shift from feeling unseen and isolated to feeling valued and respected.

A ROLE, NOT AN IDENTITY

A job is something we do, not the source of our worth or the totality of who we are. Nurturing relationships, community connections, creative pursuits, and spiritual grounding outside of work can help ensure that our sense of self-worth is not defined solely by our professional roles.

A PLACE TO PRACTICE ALIGNMENT RATHER THAN ASSIMILATION

Instead of constantly reshaping ourselves to fit environments that feel misaligned with who we are, we can look for ways to bring our values and integrity into the spaces we occupy—or seek out environments that more fully align with our values and welcome us as our full selves. While many of us may not be able to leave our primary source of income, we can consider pursuing our passions part-time. Often, when we are doing what we love, it does not feel like work.

A CONTRIBUTION, NOT JUST PRODUCTION

Rather than measuring our value only through output or productivity, we can reflect on how our work contributes to community well-being, collective progress, or a sense of purpose that extends beyond profit or performance metrics. Some organizations are expanding beyond traditional performance measures by incorporating qualitative indicators such as employee engagement, customer satisfaction, and behavioral competencies to create more holistic evaluation systems.[9]

However, bias can still exist in these systems. If you are in a role that allows you to influence how contribution and worth are measured, you may consider advocating for more equitable approaches.

REFLECTION

- How has your workplace experience shaped the way you think about your value or success?
- What messages about worth, productivity, or achievement have you internalized over time?
- Outside of your job title or professional role, what parts of your identity bring you the greatest sense of meaning or fulfillment?
- When you consider your worth beyond the workplace, what feels most central to who you are (values, practices, relationships, connections to community, spiritual grounding)?
- Are there ways your work environment has caused you to question your abilities or belonging? How might you begin to reframe those experiences through a lens of self-definition and dignity?

Restoring Your Agency: Practices for Navigating Racism at Work

Navigating racialized workplaces requires both awareness and intentional practices that protect the mind, body, and spirit while restoring power and agency. While we may not always have control over the systems we operate within, we do have choices about how we respond, how we protect ourselves, and how we maintain connection to our sense of dignity and purpose. The following practices offer ways to navigate these environments without losing yourself in the process.

Reclaiming Boundaries

Setting boundaries helps protect energy and restore balance. Questioning (and even declining) additional responsibilities that disproportionately fall on you is not selfish; it may be necessary for survival and well-being. Too often, Black employees are asked to take on extra DEI or mentoring work or expected to provide emotional support for others without recognition or compensation. If this has happened to you, you might have found yourself thinking: *I need this job. If I don't take on the additional work, I might not be considered for raises or promotions—or worse, I could be fired!*

Here are some ways to respectfully push back:

- "Thank you for considering me for these additional responsibilities. I would like to discuss how you envision they align with my current role and how we can create the time for this additional work, given my already full plate."
- "That sounds like an important initiative. Who else might be well positioned to support this so the workload is shared equitably?"
- "Before I commit, I need clarity on what responsibilities will be removed from my current workload to make space for this new task."
- "My current priorities are at capacity. If this task is essential, can we discuss reprioritizing my existing assignments?"
- "Will I be compensated for the additional work?" (If the answer is no, it gives you some additional leverage to decline.)
- "I am not sure how I would be able to assume these additional responsibilities, and I would like to respectfully decline this opportunity."
- "I want to ensure I can deliver high-quality work. Taking on more right now would compromise that, so I need to decline."

Establishing boundaries honors the principle of Ma'at, which emphasizes balance, truth, and right relationship. Protecting your time and energy is one way of restoring that balance.

Practicing Micro-Resistance

As we discussed in Chapter 5, resistance is an important component of healing Black fatigue. Janice Gassam Asare, author of *Rise and Resist*, writes, "Resistance efforts do not always have to be front and center. For most of us, our efforts to resist . . . will be quiet, subtle, and covert. . . . There are plenty of ways to resist behind the scenes."[10]

Sometimes resistance appears in small, everyday decisions: choosing when to speak, when to challenge misinformation, and when to disengage from conversations that drain your energy. Micro-resistance can also include refusing to carry the discomfort of others when difficult truths about race are raised. These small acts can help preserve dignity while resisting pressure to conform.

Reducing Emotional Labor

Black employees are often expected to educate colleagues about racism, mediate difficult conversations, or represent diverse perspectives within organizations. While this work can sometimes be meaningful, it should not be assumed or imposed. You are not responsible for educating everyone about racism or smoothing over every uncomfortable interaction. Protecting your energy may require choosing when to engage and when to step back. You might respond to requests to educate with statements like:

- "I appreciate your interest in learning more. I encourage you to explore some of the many resources available on this topic so the burden doesn't fall on colleagues."
- "I'm not in a place to take this on right now, but there are many books, articles, and trainings designed for this purpose."
- "There are experts who specialize in this work and can guide these conversations effectively. It may be more helpful to engage one of them."

Recognizing and Responding to Gaslighting

Gaslighting occurs when legitimate concerns are minimized, dismissed, or reframed as misunderstandings, overreactions, or the fault of the individual. When racism is questioned or denied, Black people may begin to doubt their own perceptions.

Recognizing when gaslighting is happening is an important first step in preventing the internalization of harmful narratives. Trusting your lived experience helps preserve clarity and confidence in environments that may attempt to undermine both.

Some examples of gaslighting include statements such as:

- "I think you're overreacting. Everyone gets treated that way sometimes."
- "I think you're misinterpreting their intentions."
- "Are you sure that actually happened? Why didn't anyone else notice?"
- "You're making this about race when it doesn't need to be."
- "Maybe if you communicated differently, this wouldn't happen."
- "I've never seen them treat anyone unfairly."

Here are some empowering responses to gaslighting:

RECENTER YOUR EXPERIENCE

- "Please respect that my experience is valid, even if it's different from yours."
- "I'm clear about what happened and how it impacted me."
- "I trust my perception of the situation."

RETURN TO THE ORIGINAL POINT

- "I want to return to the concern I raised earlier."
- "Can we stay focused on the behavior I'm addressing, please?"
- "I'm attempting to describe what happened, not debate whether it happened."

DECLINE THE ATTEMPT TO MINIMIZE

- "I feel like my experience is being dismissed."

- "Telling me I'm overreacting feels like you are minimizing a situation that is very important to me."
- "Minimizing my concerns is not helpful. I do not feel like I am being taken seriously."

SET A BOUNDARY

- "I'm not willing to have this conversation if my perspective isn't being respected."
- "If you're not able to hear me fully right now, we can revisit this later."
- "I'm not going to debate my lived experience."

NAME THE BEHAVIOR (CALMLY AND CLEARLY)

- "When my memory or intentions are questioned, it feels dismissive."
- "What I hear you saying feels like it is invalidating my experience."
- "This feels like my concerns are being reframed instead of addressed."

SHIFT ACCOUNTABILITY BACK WHERE IT BELONGS

- "I'm sharing this so the issue can be addressed, not dismissed."
- "This conversation isn't about my tone or reaction—it's about the behavior that occurred."
- "I'm asking you to also consider and listen to the impact, not just the intent."

AFFIRM YOUR NEEDS

- "I need this concern to be acknowledged, not explained away."
- "I need a conversation grounded in respect, not dismissal."
- "I need us to talk about the behavior rather than whether I interpreted it correctly."

CHOOSE DISENGAGEMENT WHEN NEEDED

- "This doesn't feel productive right now, so I'm stepping away from the conversation."
- "I'm going to pause this discussion for my well-being."
- "I'm ending this conversation because if feels invalidating."

Documenting incidents, seeking support from trusted colleagues, or raising concerns in spaces where accountability is more likely can help counter attempts to dismiss or distort what occurred.

Not every situation requires direct confrontation. Sometimes protecting your energy may mean choosing when to engage and when to disengage. The goal is not to convince someone determined to deny your experience, but to remain grounded in your own truth.

Restoring the Village at Work

Even within challenging workplaces, it is possible to build micro-villages that create spaces of support and solidarity with colleagues who share similar experiences or values. These may include affinity groups, mentorship networks, "sista-friend" or "brotha-friend" circles, or what some people describe as a personal board of directors. Remember, while employee resource groups can provide connection and visibility, they may also face limitations imposed by institutional rules that prevent true communal care (as discussed in Chapter 4).

Protecting the Spirit During Conflict

Workplace conflict and racial tension can take a toll on emotional and spiritual well-being. Practices like those described in Chapter 8, such as breathing, reflection, prayer, meditation, or grounding, can help reconnect us to our inner strength during difficult moments. For many people, drawing on ancestral wisdom and spiritual traditions provides a deeper sense of guidance and resilience (see Chapter 7). These practices remind us that our strength is rooted in something larger than any single workplace experience.

Redefining Success

We live in a capitalistic society where success is often defined by how much money you make, the number of degrees that you have, what title you hold, and other subjective measures. But who sets these standards?

Success does not have to mean constant advancement or external validation. It can mean alignment with one's values, dignity, and well-being. For some, success may mean maintaining balance between work, family, community, and spiritual life. Reclaiming this definition allows individuals to resist narrow measures of worth that prioritize productivity above humanity and can help alleviate Black fatigue.

Knowing When to Leave

Sometimes the most powerful act of resistance is departure. Recognizing when a workplace is no longer aligned with your well-being can be an important step in protecting your long-term health and dignity. Leaving an environment that consistently diminishes you is an act of self-preservation, not a failure. Of course, while this sounds good on paper, economic realities may make it difficult.

It's often useful to develop contingency plans for the future, in case your current employment situation changes. This can happen for any number of reasons: you get laid off, you're reassigned and do not like the new job, or you're under constant stress or feel undervalued and decide you need to make a change. You may not be able to leave in the short term, but developing an exit plan and working toward those goals can provide a sense of direction and agency. In the meantime, the strategies outlined in this chapter can help you survive until you can actualize your alternatives.

Exploring Alternative Pathways

Reclaiming power, agency, and voice may involve exploring alternative career pathways. Entrepreneurship, cooperative ventures, and mission-driven work can offer opportunities that align labor with purpose, community impact, and personal values.

Collective Advocacy

While individual strategies are important, many workplace challenges are structural rather than personal. Collective advocacy through organizing, coalition building, or coordinated action can help shift workplace cultures and policies. Working in community with others reflects a long tradition of collective resistance within Black communities, where progress has often been achieved not through individual effort alone, but through shared action and solidarity.

REFLECTION

- Which of the practices described here feels most relevant to your current workplace experience? What might it look like to begin implementing that practice in a way that protects your well-being?
- Are there areas in your work life where clearer boundaries could help restore balance or protect your energy?
- What forms of resistance help restore you during your workday?
- Who are the people in your workplace or professional network who could be part of your "micro-village," offering support, affirmation, or shared advocacy?
- Are there moments when you may have internalized harmful workplace narratives or expectations? How might reclaiming your agency shift how you respond in the future?
- How might drawing on the resilience and collective wisdom of those who came before you influence how you navigate challenges in your workplace today?
- Where are you choosing survival over wholeness?
- What would a work environment aligned with your spirit look like?

Summary

Navigating workplaces, particularly those shaped by dominant cultural norms, requires courage, discernment, and community. Returning to wholeness at work is itself a form of resistance and survival. Agency, power, and voice can be reclaimed through alignment, boundaries, and the restoration of the village. These practices help Black people maintain a sense of self, protect their spirit, and navigate imperfect systems without sacrificing their wholeness. The goal is not merely to survive within racialized workplaces, but to cultivate sustainability, dignity, and joy.

While it can be difficult to set boundaries and say no in work situations, do not assume that it is impossible or that you must continue to endure environments that do not value you for who you are and the unique contributions you bring.

Part III

HEALING PRACTICES FOR DAILY RENEWAL

Healing is a reminder of what we already are and what we have always been part of.

—Resmaa Menakem,
American author and psychotherapist[1]

SEVEN

CALLING ON THE ANCESTORS

I go forth along, and stand as ten thousand.

—Maya Angelou, American memoirist, essayist, poet, and civil rights activist[2]

Author's Note: This chapter is written in Mary Frances's voice.

I have been living in Barbados, West Indies, part time for four years now. During this time, my curiosity about the wider Caribbean deepened, and I decided to get a taste of more of the islands on a recent cruise. The ship sailed the Southern Caribbean, including the islands of St. Lucia, Montserrat, Antigua, St. Kitts and Nevis, St. Martin, Martinique, Tortola, Bequia, and Grenada. I wanted to understand the histories of these islands and how their cultures are interconnected yet distinct. It was an educational and enlightening experience. One theme emerged on every island during the historical tours: a profound reverence for the past and a deep veneration for the ancestors.

This chapter is intended to describe, based on my personal experiences, how individuals, groups, and cultures call on ancestors today and the importance of this practice for healing Black fatigue. Calling on the ancestors can expand our sense of belonging and reconnect us to the wisdom that sustains us across generations. Who are our ancestors? They could be blood—parents, grandparents, lineage known and unknown. Or they might be communal—activists, healers, thinkers, protectors, and others who've shaped Black life. They might be spiritual or ancestral archetypes, or simply those we choose or "adopt." My recent cruise experience allowed me to embrace a more inclusive, expansive idea of the notion of ancestor.

In St. Lucia, our guide shared proudly, "Before we go to the doctor, we ask our grandmothers for the best remedy for our maladies." That simple statement illustrated how the importance of ancestral wisdom endures.

In Nevis, Alexander Hamilton's birthplace, the guide was categorical in his assertion that Hamilton was born to a mixed-race mother, even though most sources claim that there is no proof of that and that it is unlikely.[3] (Note: The original portrayer of Hamilton in the hit musical was Lin-Manuel Miranda, a brown-skinned Puerto Rican.) Although there is controversy about Hamilton's ethnicity, remembering and recounting the possibility of this different, even if unproven, narrative is important.

In Tortola, the Fahie Hill/Ridge Road mural project, initiated in 2001, recounts the island's cultural and historical past.[4] The twenty-three connected panels tell the story of everyday life in the British Virgin Islands in the 1950s, before modern conveniences transformed island society. It is a breathtaking scene, capturing one historical point in time never to be forgotten or minimized.

During my time in Grenada, I visited a spice and herb garden where the guide shared the medicinal properties of staples like nutmeg, cinnamon, bay leaf, ginger, and turmeric. Walking through the garden, I was reminded how these plants carry generations of inherited wisdom. Learning about these remedies felt like being reintroduced to an ancestral pharmacy, one rooted in the earth and maintained through memory, practice, and cultural transmission. In this way, the spice garden was not just a lesson in horticulture but a reminder that calling on the ancestors often begins with listening to the teachings embedded in the land itself.

Across the region, this inherited knowledge supports not only physical healing but also spiritual discernment and practical insight for everyday living. These ideals echo the concept of the extended self described in Part I, which encompasses the living, the unborn, and the ancestors. Ancestral consciousness becomes a form of spiritual grounding, or Sakhu, as discussed previously, and ancestral remembrance becomes a pathway toward truth, balance, and right relationship (Ma'at).

Jaslyn's Uncle Felix and Aunt Gwen

I was also reminded of the significance of ancestors through the story of my dear friend, Jaslyn, who was born and lived her early years in Barbados but spent most of her adult life living in Australia and other parts of the world. Fifteen years ago, she returned to Barbados to care for elderly relatives, including her beloved Uncle Felix, who lived to be 102, and his wife, her Aunt Gwen. After Felix's passing, she remained in another family home until it was recently sold, which left her unsure of where to relocate.

For months, she searched, hoping to find a place that fit her spirit and her budget, but nothing felt quite right. Eventually, she found herself drawn back to her aunt and uncle's small chattel house—the same home where she had lived for a time as a young child. Chattel houses were prevalent among plantation workers in Barbados after slavery was abolished in 1838. By law, workers owned the structures but not the land on which they stood, and in some cases that separation of ownership still requires occupants to navigate a legal process to secure title to the land.

These homes were designed to be easily dismantled, moved, and reassembled. This made it possible to relocate them if their owners changed jobs or were evicted by a plantation owner. Their very architecture tells a story of resilience, mobility, and innovation under often oppressive conditions.

Aunt Gwen had predeceased Uncle Felix, and he had continued living in the chattel house until his death, with Jaslyn his primary caretaker. On his one-hundredth birthday she organized a streetwide celebration in his honor, securing permission to block off the road so neighbors, friends, and community members could gather. It was a joyful outpouring of love and remembrance, a living tribute to his life and legacy.

Deciding to renovate the chattel house became more than a housing solution for my friend; it became an act of devotion, a way of keeping her relatives' memory alive. She is reviving not only a structure, but a lineage.

To me, her story is a profound example of honoring ancestors. By choosing to restore her aunt and uncle's home, she is restoring connection, identity, and continuity. She is practicing ancestral remembrance as a lived, embodied commitment.

REFLECTION

- Who are the ancestors you call on?
- Which qualities or strengths have been passed down to you?
- How might calling on ancestors support you when you feel fatigue, grief, or misalignment?

Practices for Calling on the Ancestors

There are many practices you can embrace to honor your ancestors. We offer a few examples here, with additional practices shared in Chapter 8. You can also explore the *Black Fatigue* website (blackfatigue.com) for further ideas. Each practice is an invitation, not homework or a prescription.

While the specific language and expressions may vary, ancestor remembrance is present across many traditions, including Judaism, Christianity, Islam, Buddhism, Indigenous and African spiritual systems, and more. Even in traditions that pray exclusively to a God, remembering foremothers and forefathers, saints, elders, or martyrs is a common and respected practice. Let what feels right to you and aligns with your faith guide how you engage, whether with all, some, or none of these practices.

Libation: Water as a Bridge

When we pour water, we acknowledge the ones who made our lives possible—those we know by name and those whose names have been taken from us. A small bowl or glass is enough. Speak aloud (or silently) as you pour:

"I pour for those who came before me. I pour for the named and the unnamed. I pour for guidance, clarity, and remembrance."

Let the act be simple and sincere. The point is relationship, not performance.

Ancestral Altar

An altar can be as simple as a corner of a shelf, a windowsill, or the top of a dresser. Place on the altar a candle or small light, a glass of water, a photo or other symbol of someone you honor, and a natural element—stone, leaf, shell, or earth. Add what feels right over time: a swatch of cloth, a handwritten prayer, a sprig of herbs from the garden. Visit this place daily, even if only for thirty seconds. The regularity more than the length of your visits builds connection.

Morning Supplication

Offer a morning remembrance of the ancestors, such as "May I walk in the strength of those who came before me today." These words can be an affirmation of belonging and continuity, and an acknowledgment that your life is rooted in those who came before you.

This practice is not intended to replace or conflict with prayer rituals based on your faith. It is offered as a complementary practice of remembrance and grounding.

Ancestral Journaling

Choose one prompt and linger with it for a week:

- Which ancestor (named or unnamed) stood up for me today?
- What trait did I inherit that protects me?
- What can I return to the lineage (with gratitude) that is not mine to carry anymore?

Let your answers be brief, even a sentence. Consistency creates depth.

Story Circles

Story circles, described more fully in Chapter 8, are gatherings of family or community to share stories of elders or ancestors. Here are some examples of questions you might explore in the circle:

- Who was the first ancestor who taught you something important?
- What do you know (or sense) about what your ancestors carried?
- What "adopted ancestor"—such as an activist, thinker, elder, teacher, or other ancestral archetype—shaped you, and how?

Somatic Practices

Resmaa Menakem activates the wisdom of elders in his work. A best-selling author and leading voice on racialized trauma, he is the creator of the concept of Somatic Abolitionism, which utilizes the body and its natural resilience as mechanisms for healing racialized trauma. He suggests a number of practices inspired by his work and included in his book *My Grandmother's Hands*, such as settling the body before calling on the elders (see the breathing and body mapping exercises we outline in Chapter 8), remembering the plight of the ancestors (asking, *What did my people do to survive? What strengths did they place in my bones?*), and holding a meaningful object (such as a stone, shell, scrap of fabric) with intention and feeling the sensations that arise.[5]

In essence, Menakem teaches us that the body is the access point to ancestral wisdom. By settling, sensing, remembering, and inviting connection, people can tap into lineage resources for clarity, grounding, and resilience.

Rhythm as Medicine

Menakem says gentle repetition can repair frayed edges in the nervous system. Try humming, rocking, tapping your heart space, or a few minutes of soft drumming. Speak an ancestor's name on the exhale. Let your body find a steady tempo. Rhythm makes room for steadiness; steadiness makes room for clarity.

As a living example, an all-female drumming group was recently formed in Barbados, inspired by Giwayen Mata in Atlanta, Georgia. (*Giwayen Mata* is a Hausa term from Nigeria that translates to "Elephant Women." It is used to denote leadership, strength, wisdom, and the nurturing of a multigenerational community.) In a newspaper piece about the Barbadian group, called the Drum Sisters Collective: Ola Ilè (a name from Yoruba meaning women of honor, dignity, and ancestral wealth, grounded in the legacy of African womanhood), members were asked what inspired them to join. One said, "I have always been deeply moved by the sound of the drum. It resonates with me, filling my soul with joy and pride of my ancestral heritage." The author of the newspaper article summed it up this way: "For many, the drum is ancestral memory made audible."[6]

REFLECTION

- Why is it important to you personally to remember and call on the ancestors?
- Which practices resonate with you?
- What other practices are important to you, and how can you share and or experience them with others?

Summary

Calling on the ancestors is in itself a healing act. It heals by:

RESTORING CONTINUITY In a world that often fragments identity, ancestral remembrance reconnects us to a lineage of strength, creativity, and survival.

EXPANDING BELONGING We are reminded that we are never alone; we walk with a vast community of forbears whose lives made ours possible.

PROVIDING EMBODIED WISDOM Many ancestral practices, such as plant medicine, prayer, movement, and storytelling, activate the nervous system's pathways of safety and regulation, offering grounding in moments of fatigue or stress.

REFRAMING RESILIENCE Resilience is often thought of as simply "enduring" or finding ways to "put up with" harm, but our ancestors teach us something deeper. Remembering them reminds us that resilience is really about discernment, resistance, and the refusal to accept injustice as normal or inevitable.

INVITING SPIRITUAL ALIGNMENT Calling on the ancestors is a return to balance, to Ma'at—an opportunity to realign with truth, purpose, and right relationship with self and community.

Across the Caribbean, I witnessed how ancestral reverence is a living, breathing form of healing. And in embracing that consciousness, we, too, can find a deeper sense of who we are in the continuum of past, present, and future. Of course, my experience is just one small example of how we can remember, revere, and embrace ancestral wisdom. As mentioned previously, other cultures beyond those of African descent also have practices that include calling on the ancestors; I invite you to explore them.

EIGHT

HEALING PRACTICES FOR THE MIND, BODY, AND SPIRIT

If you surrendered to the air, you could ride it.

—Toni Morrison, American novelist and Nobel Laureate[1]

Black fatigue can shape our thoughts, emotions, and sense of mental well-being. It is carried in our bodies through chronic stress, physical exhaustion, and sustained tension, affecting our health and vitality. It can also impact how connected we feel to ourselves, our purpose, and the people around us. In other words, Black fatigue is experienced across the whole self: mind, body, and spirit. This means healing, too, must address the whole self.

Contrary to traditional Western approaches, many African and Indigenous traditions have long understood well-being as both holistic and communal, recognizing that balance and alignment require care for all parts of our being, as well as the relationships that sustain us.

Drawn from African-centered and Indigenous wisdom, spiritual traditions, and lived experience, the practices in this chapter offer simple ways to begin restoring that balance. They are invitations rather than prescriptions, providing practical ways to return to wholeness, and are not meant to be done perfectly or all in one sitting.

This chapter is designed as a guide you can return to whenever you need to reconnect with breath, movement, reflection, moments of joy, spirit, or the support of your village. While many of these practices are intended for adults, as we discuss in *Black Fatigue*, young people are not immune to the impacts of racism and also need spaces for healing. We encourage you to find ways to introduce some of these practices to the children and youth in your lives, creating opportunities for healing, reflection, and connection across generations.

Healing the Body

Black fatigue manifests emotionally, mentally, and physically. The stress of navigating racialized environments can show up in the body through tension, illness, anxiety, and other signs of nervous system overload. Over time, these physical responses become so familiar that we normalize them and begin to ignore them.

Healing the body begins with bringing awareness back to it, noticing when and how Black fatigue manifests and creating moments to reset. The practices in this section offer simple ways to reconnect with breath, movement, and rest. They are designed to help the body release tension, regulate the nervous system, and restore a greater sense of balance.

REFLECTION BEFORE PRACTICE

- How does your body feel when you're tense, tired, or energized?
- Are there specific places in your body where you typically notice tightness, heaviness, or fatigue?
- When you experience stress or are overwhelmed, where do you tend to feel it most in your body?
- What signals does your body give you when it needs rest, movement, or care?
- When was the last time your body felt fully relaxed, safe, or at ease?

Body Mapping: Noticing Where Black Fatigue Lives

PURPOSE: TO BUILD AWARENESS OF WHERE BLACK FATIGUE LIVES IN THE BODY

Before we can begin healing Black fatigue in the body, we must first understand how it is carried within us. Trauma therapist Resmaa Menakem reminds us that racialized trauma is often held physically (see Chapter 7).[2] Becoming aware of sensations such as tension, tightness, or fatigue can be an important first step in healing.

Some manifestations of fatigue and stress include tight or raised shoulders, jaw tension, headaches, stomach discomfort, and persistent tiredness. In some cases, the long-term impact of stress can also contribute to more serious health concerns, including heart conditions, diabetes, and obesity.

Many people move through their day disconnected from their physical selves. Being in tune with our bodies helps us recognize what needs care and when. This body mapping practice is an invitation to reconnect with your body from head to toe and notice where tension, heaviness, or discomfort may be present.

WHEN TO USE THIS PRACTICE

We recommend using this practice regularly and before engaging in the others in this chapter. Return to it often as a check-in to see where you may still be holding Black fatigue in your body.

HOW TO PRACTICE

Find a comfortable position, either sitting or lying down, in a quiet space free from distraction. Close your eyes or lower your gaze, and allow your attention to turn inward.

- Take a few slow, deep breaths, inhaling through your nose and exhaling through your mouth. Notice the rise and fall of your chest and stomach. With each breath, allow your shoulders and body to soften.
- Take a moment to feel where your body is making contact with the chair, floor, or bed.

- Now begin to slowly scan your body from head to toe. As you move your attention through different areas, simply notice without judgment any sensations that are present—tension, heaviness, fatigue, warmth, or ease. You may choose to gently place a hand on different parts of your body as you scan, or to take a slow, deep breath into any area that feels tight or tired.
- Continue moving your awareness gradually through your body, noticing what you feel in your feet, legs, hips, abdomen, back, chest, shoulders, arms, neck, and head.
- Finally, take a moment to sense your body as a whole.
- When you feel ready, gently open your eyes or look up and return your attention to the room. You may wish to stretch or move slowly before you get up.

REFLECTION

- How did the body scan make you feel?
- What surprised you?

Orienting Pause: Reconnecting with the Present

PURPOSE: TO HELP THE BODY RECOGNIZE SAFETY IN THE PRESENT MOMENT

Black fatigue can place the body in a constant state of vigilance. Navigating racism in everyday life often requires heightened awareness and emotional regulation, which can lead to tension or overstimulation. Over time, the body may become accustomed to this pattern, remaining on high alert even when there is no immediate threat. The orienting pause is a simple practice that helps us recognize safety in the present moment, allowing the body to begin to settle.

WHEN TO USE THIS PRACTICE

You might try an orienting pause when you notice one or more of the following signs:

- Tension in your shoulders or jaw
- Shallow or rushed breathing
- Feeling overstimulated or on edge
- Difficulty focusing or settling your thoughts

These can be signals that your body needs a moment to reset.

HOW TO PRACTICE

Pause for a moment and slowly look around the space where you are. Notice what is in your environment:

- What colors do you see?
- What shapes or objects stand out to you?
- What sounds do you hear nearby?

Feel your feet on the ground and, if seated, how your body is supported. Allow your breath to slow naturally as you take in your surroundings. Continue this observation until you feel your body relax.

Even a brief pause like this can help the body release some of the tension it has been carrying.

REFLECTION

- What do you notice in your body after taking a moment to pause and orient yourself to your surroundings?

Breath Reset: Returning the Body to Balance

PURPOSE: TO USE BREATH TO CALM THE BODY AND RESTORE BALANCE

Breathwork is a helpful practice for settling the body's response to stress. Slowing your breath can help reduce muscle tension, slow your heart rate, and shift your body out of a state of vigilance. Intentional breathing can also create a feeling of physical grounding and calm. Breathing techniques have been used for thousands of years in many healing traditions, including Ayurvedic and traditional Chinese medicine, to support balance in both the body and mind.

WHEN TO USE THIS PRACTICE

This practice may be helpful when you are experiencing high levels of stress or anxiety, or when you are processing feelings of grief, trauma, or intense emotions. Breathwork can also be useful just before bed to prepare your body for rest.

HOW TO PRACTICE

There are many forms of breathwork, including diaphragmatic (belly) breathing, box breathing, and 4-7-8 breathing, as well as other more intensive practices that are sometimes facilitated by trained practitioners. Here we offer an example of box breathing, a simple technique often used to regulate the body's fight-or-flight response during moments of stress.

- Begin with a deep exhale, releasing the air in your lungs.
- *Inhale:* Slowly breathe in through your nose while counting to four.
- *Hold:* Hold your breath for a count of four.
- *Exhale:* Slowly breathe out through your nose or mouth for a count of four.
- *Hold:* Hold your breath while your lungs are empty for a count of four.

Continue this cycle for three to five minutes, or until your body feels more settled. It might be helpful to visualize a square or trace the shape of a square with your finger as you move through each step of the practice.

REFLECTION

- What changes do you notice in your body after slowing your breath?

Rhythm Reset: Renewal Through Movement

PURPOSE: TO RELEASE TENSION AND RENEW BALANCE THROUGH MOVEMENT AND RHYTHM

As we've mentioned throughout this book, movement and rhythm have long been part of African and diasporic traditions of expression, resilience, and healing. From dance and drumming (see Chapter 7) to spirituals and collective song (see Chapter 5), rhythm has long provided ways for people to process emotions, relieve stress, and reconnect with joy.

Through movement, we can release tension and stagnant energy and begin to restore balance and dignity. Research supports that movement can help the body process stress and regulate emotional responses.[3]

WHEN TO USE THIS PRACTICE

This practice may be helpful when you sense tension building in your body, when your energy feels low, or when you need a moment to reconnect with joy and aliveness. Movement can be especially helpful after a stressful experience, as a break during long periods of sitting or working, or whenever your body is asking for release (revisit the body mapping practice to help identify what your body may need).

HOW TO PRACTICE

There are many ways to incorporate movement and rhythm into your day. The goal is to allow your body to move in ways that feel natural and freeing. This might look like:

- Swaying gently to music
- Stretching your arms, shoulders, or back
- Dancing to your favorite song
- Tapping your feet or clapping your hands to a rhythm
- Taking a walk outside
- Engaging in exercise or somatic movement

Remember, the movement doesn't need to be structured or perfect. Just enjoy yourself! Even a few minutes of intentional movement can help shift energy and release tension in the body, making space for moments of lightness, pleasure, and joy.

REFLECTION

- What shifts did you notice in your body after allowing it to move?
- How can you incorporate more movement into your daily routine?

Micro Joys to Sustain Us Through Macro Fatigue

PURPOSE: TO RECONNECT THE BODY TO PLEASURE AND ALIVENESS

Joy can feel distant or unattainable when we are experiencing Black fatigue. Yet even the smallest moments of beauty and pleasure can reawaken the senses and create a pathway toward renewal and healing.

Business and marketing coach Glo Atanmo says "micro joys are how we survive macro grief."[4] Micro joys are small, intentional moments that sustain us through ongoing and collective fatigue. They can reconnect us to ease in the midst of everyday life, and they help nourish the body and spirit. Micro joys remind us that moments of happiness are not luxuries; they are a necessity. As bell hooks often wrote, the practice of choosing joy and love in the midst of struggle can itself be a radical act of reclaiming our humanity.

We recognize that joy does not erase the realities of living through racism, but it reminds us that our spirits were not meant to live only in reaction to harm. As we discussed in Chapter 5, practicing joy can help sustain us for the long journey of confronting injustice. Micro joys are one way we nourish the spirit so that resistance remains possible.

WHEN TO USE THIS PRACTICE

This practice can be helpful when the weight of Black fatigue feels overwhelming, and joy feels out of reach. It's the perfect reminder that beauty and ease still exist in the world around you. Opening yourself to micro joys can be practiced at any time throughout the day.

HOW TO PRACTICE

Micro joy moments may look like:

- Honoring your capacity by canceling plans and feeling relief
- Putting your phone down and noticing the stillness and quiet around you
- Being understood without having to explain yourself
- Seeing your pet's excitement when you arrive home
- Listening to music that meets your mood instead of trying to fix it
- Hearing a song that reminds you of home or your childhood
- Stretching your body and feeling it soften
- Walking outside and noticing something beautiful—a flower, an animal, the sunset

- Planting or tending herbs and plants that connect you to your ancestors
- Laughing freely in a space where your joy feels unpoliced
- Acts of kindness, love, unity, and respect
- Remembering you've survived something hard before
- Moving your body—dancing, swaying, or feeling rhythm in whatever way feels right
- Sending a thank you note or thinking of you text to someone just because

Micro joys help us counterbalance macro fatigue, not by fixing everything, but by giving us a little relief, energy, and pause. You might consider creating a list of your own micro joys to return to and add to over time.

REFLECTION

- Which of the micro joys in the previous list resonated with you?
- What would you add to your own list?
- What is one small moment of joy you will intentionally create today?

Sacred Rest: Honoring the Body's Need to Restore Itself

PURPOSE: TO HONOR THE BODY'S NEED FOR RESTORATION AND RENEWAL

Historically, Black bodies have been overworked and denied rest and restoration. From enslavement through generations of labor exploitation, exhaustion has often been normalized as a condition of survival. Yet rest is part of being human, not something we should have to earn.

As we discussed in Chapter 5, theologian and activist Tricia Hersey (founder of The Nap Ministry) has written about rest as a powerful challenge to cultures that equate human worth with constant productivity.[5] Choosing rest is not simply about preparing to do more; it is an affirmation of our humanity in a world that has too often denied Black bodies the right to pause, restore, and simply be.

Rest does not always mean sleep. It can also include moments of stillness, quiet, and slowing down—small pauses that allow the body and mind to recover.

WHEN TO USE THIS PRACTICE

This practice may be helpful when you notice signs of exhaustion in your body, when your energy feels depleted, or when you recognize that you have been moving through the day without pause. If the body mapping practice earlier in this chapter helped you notice areas of tension, heaviness, or fatigue, sacred rest can be a way to respond to those signals with care. It can be practiced at any time—during a break in your day, before sleep, or whenever your body signals the need to slow down.

HOW TO PRACTICE

Sacred rest can take many forms. The goal is not to achieve perfect stillness, but to create space for the body to relax and recover. This might include:

- Stepping away from activity for a few minutes
- Lying down or sitting quietly
- Closing your eyes and allowing your body to settle
- Setting aside intentional time for rest during the day
- Creating small pockets of stillness between activities
- Setting boundaries around time, energy, and expectations
- Ending your workday at a reasonable time
- Ensuring you get enough hours of sleep for deep restoration

Even brief moments of rest can help the body reset and remind us that we are not meant to move through life in constant exhaustion. At times, sacred rest may simply mean honoring the body's need for sleep and allowing ourselves the dignity of full restoration.

REFLECTION

- What would it look like to give your body the sacred rest it needs today?

Healing the Mind

Black fatigue can weigh heavily on the mind. Constant vigilance, navigating bias, and carrying the emotional impact of racism may lead to mental exhaustion, self-doubt, and internalized pressure. Over time, these experiences can shape how we interpret situations, the stories we tell ourselves, and what we believe we must carry alone.

Healing the mind involves creating space to pause, reflect, and realign with what is true. The practices in this section invite you to slow down, examine your thoughts, and reconnect with a sense of balance and self-compassion. They are designed to help the mind find clarity, challenge harmful narratives, and reconnect with truth, balance, and inner alignment.

REFLECTION BEFORE PRACTICE

- What thoughts or worries feel most present for you right now?
- Are there expectations—internal or external—that feel heavy to carry?
- In what moments do you notice your mind becoming overwhelmed or fatigued?
- What helps you regain clarity when your thoughts feel scattered or heavy?

Sakhu Reflection: Returning to Alignment

PURPOSE: TO CULTIVATE CLARITY AND ALIGNMENT BY RECONNECTING WITH ONE'S INNER TRUTH AND DISCERNMENT

As introduced in Chapter 2, the concept of Sakhu in African-centered psychology refers to the illumination of the spirit and the alignment of one's deeper truth. When external pressures accumulate and exacerbate Black fatigue, it can become difficult to distinguish between what is truly ours to carry and what has been imposed upon us by external expectations, systems, and environments. This short reflection invites us to pause, reconnect with our inner knowing, and return to alignment with our truth.

WHEN TO USE THIS PRACTICE

This practice may be helpful when you feel mentally overwhelmed, conflicted about a decision, or unsure of whether the expectations placed upon you align with your values or well-being. It can also serve as a daily moment of reflection to restore clarity and perspective.

HOW TO PRACTICE

At the beginning or end of each day, ask yourself:

- What is true?
- What is aligned?
- What is mine to carry today?

Write your responses in a journal or sit quietly with the questions. Pairing the reflection with a few slow, deep breaths can help in settling the mind. Reflecting on these questions in real time as you navigate a difficult situation can help bring calm and grounding.

REFLECTION

- What expectations or burdens can you release today?

Reframing with Ancestral Wisdom: Reclaiming the Narrative

PURPOSE: TO CHALLENGE LIMITING NARRATIVES AND RECONNECT WITH THE STRENGTH, PERSPECTIVE, AND WISDOM DRAWN FROM OUR ANCESTORS AND CULTURAL TRADITIONS

Racism often shapes the narratives about us. There are stories imposed upon us and stories we may begin to tell ourselves. These are not narratives we are meant to carry or embody. Internalized messages may include the idea that we need to constantly prove our worth or belonging. Healing Black fatigue invites us to release these narratives and choose ones grounded in dignity, truth, and possibility. African and diasporic traditions hold generations of wisdom about resilience and dignity. Drawing on the insight of our ancestors can help us reframe limiting narratives and reclaim a fuller understanding of who we are.

WHEN TO USE THIS PRACTICE

This practice may be helpful when you notice yourself internalizing limiting beliefs or narratives about your worth, belonging, or capability. It invites you to pause and consider how the wisdom and resilience of those who came before you might offer a different perspective.

HOW TO PRACTICE

Reflect on recurring self-limiting thoughts and pause and question the narrative. Ask yourself:

- Where did this story come from?
- Why do I believe it is true?
- What would my ancestors or elders say about the situation?

Then replace the narrative with one grounded in dignity and truth.

For example, here are some narratives we often internalize and potential reframes:

"I have to be strong all the time."	→	"Strength can also look like resting, asking for help, and not carrying everything alone."
"I have to be twice as good."	→	"My worth isn't measured by overperformance."
"I don't belong here."	→	"I belong because I am."

REFLECTION

- What new story about yourself feels more aligned with dignity and truth? Repeat that story to yourself daily.

Naming and Releasing: Setting Down What We Carry

PURPOSE: TO ACKNOWLEDGE AND RELEASE EMOTIONAL BURDENS THAT WERE NEVER MEANT TO BE CARRIED INDEFINITELY

Black fatigue involves carrying unspoken emotional weight. Naming and releasing those emotions can reduce their intensity and create space for greater ease and clarity. Releasing them does not mean ignoring reality; it means refusing to hold onto what harms us and moving forward with greater awareness.

WHEN TO USE THIS PRACTICE

This practice may be helpful when you notice emotional burdens building up, such as anger, frustration, grief, or expectations that feel heavy to carry. Naming these feelings and consciously releasing them can help create space for relief and renewal.

HOW TO PRACTICE

Pause and identify what you are feeling.

- Name the specific emotion or emotions (e.g., anger, exhaustion, sadness, frustration).
- Write or speak them aloud.

You may also choose a symbolic way to release your emotional burden. For example, pairing this practice with breathwork, as you breathe in, invite in a positive or grounding emotion, such as calm, peace, or strength. As you breathe out, name the emotion you are releasing, as in "I release anger" or "I let go of frustration." Repeat this cycle several times until you feel more grounded.

If you write the emotion on a piece of paper, you may choose to tear it up, burn it, or discard it as a symbolic act of letting go.

REFLECTION

- What do you notice differently in your mind after releasing these emotions?

Healing the Spirit

Beyond the body and mind, Black fatigue can also affect the spirit. When the weight of injustice and daily stress accumulates, it can leave us feeling disconnected from our purpose, joy, and the deeper sources of strength that sustain us.

As we have mentioned throughout the book, across many African and diasporic traditions, spiritual well-being is rooted in connection to ancestors, community, and a sense of meaning greater than ourselves. The practices in this section offer ways to nurture that connection and restore alignment, gratitude, and spiritual grounding. They are designed to help restore spiritual balance by reconnecting us with our values, our ancestors, and the relationships that sustain and guide us.

REFLECTION BEFORE PRACTICE

- When do you feel most connected to your purpose or deeper sense of meaning?
- What experiences help you feel spiritually grounded or aligned?
- Are there moments when Black fatigue has made you feel disconnected from joy or hope?
- What practices, traditions, or memories help restore your spirit?

Ma'at Alignment Check: Returning to Balance

PURPOSE: TO RECONNECT WITH THE GUIDING PRINCIPLES OF TRUTH, BALANCE, JUSTICE, AND HARMONY AND RESTORE SPIRITUAL ALIGNMENT

In Chapter 2, we introduced the concept of Ma'at—truth, balance, harmony, reciprocity, and justice. Black fatigue is the consequence of living in systems that routinely violate Ma'at. Returning to the guiding principles of Ma'at can restore spiritual alignment and clarity. These principles offer a way to pause and examine whether the choices we make, and the environments we navigate, support our well-being and dignity. Living in alignment with our values strengthens our resilience.

WHEN TO USE THIS PRACTICE

This practice may be helpful when you are feeling morally conflicted, spiritually unsettled, or unsure about how to respond to a situation. It invites you to pause and reflect on whether your actions, choices, and environment are aligned with the values that guide your life.

You might use this practice when:

- Facing a difficult decision
- Navigating conflict or injustice
- Feeling disconnected from your sense of purpose
- Needing clarity about what integrity looks like in a particular moment

HOW TO PRACTICE

On a piece of paper, create a simple chart. Across the top, write the guiding principles: Truth, Balance, Harmony, Reciprocity, and Justice. Along the side, write two categories: My Actions and My Environment. Table 6 shows what this might look like.

- In each box, briefly note ways your actions and/or environment reflect these principles.
- Notice where alignment already exists and where something feels out of balance.
- Reflect on whether there are small shifts that could help restore greater alignment.

Table 6. An example Ma'at alignment chart

	TRUTH	BALANCE	HARMONY	RECIPROCITY	JUSTICE
My Actions					
My Environment					

REFLECTION

- Which of these principles is asking for more attention in your life right now?

Ancestral Presence Visualization: Remembering We Are Not Alone

PURPOSE: TO CULTIVATE GUIDANCE, PROTECTION, AND CONNECTION BY CALLING ON THE WISDOM AND PRESENCE OF THE ANCESTORS

Throughout this book, and specifically in Chapter 7, we discuss how honoring the presence of our ancestors is deeply rooted in African and diasporic traditions. In many of these traditions, ancestors are viewed as an ongoing presence in our lives, not distant figures from the past. They represent lineage, strength, and continuity. Remembering those who came before us can provide guidance and encouragement as we navigate difficult times.

WHEN TO USE THIS PRACTICE

This practice may be helpful when you are feeling alone, discouraged, or uncertain about the path ahead, or perhaps when you are navigating a difficult conversation, a challenging experience at work, or a health concern. Visualizing the presence of ancestors can remind us that we are part of a larger lineage of resilience, wisdom, and care. Connecting with our ancestors can restore a sense of belonging and confidence.

HOW TO PRACTICE

Sit quietly and close your eyes.

- Visualize ancestors, elders, or lineage figures who represent strength and guidance.

- Imagine their presence surrounding you and offering support.
- Reflect on the strength carried through generations.

You may choose to focus on one specific ancestor or a group of ancestors. You may visualize them standing around or beside you, offering strength and encouragement. This practice pairs well with meditation or prayer. You may also express this visualization through drawing or journaling.

See Chapter 7 for additional practices that call on the ancestors.

REFLECTION

- What wisdom or encouragement did your ancestors offer you today?

Gratitude Ritual: Honoring What Sustains Us

PURPOSE: TO CULTIVATE APPRECIATION FOR THE PEOPLE, EXPERIENCES, AND RESOURCES THAT SUPPORT AND UPLIFT US

Studies have shown that expressing gratitude physically rewires our brains, making us naturally more positive.[6] Gratitude has many beneficial health effects, including greater emotional and social well-being, better sleep, lower risk of depression, and favorable markers of cardiovascular health.[7] In the context of healing Black fatigue, gratitude does not deny injustice or hardship; it helps us recognize and appreciate what continues to sustain us. In many African-centered traditions, gratitude is also a way of honoring relationships with one another, with our ancestors, and with the world around us. In this way, it supports the balance and interconnectedness reflected in principles such as Ma'at and Ubuntu.

WHEN TO USE THIS PRACTICE

This practice may be helpful when you want to shift your attention to what sustains you, even during difficult moments. Gratitude rituals can help restore balance and remind us that moments of care and connection still exist alongside struggle.

HOW TO PRACTICE

At the start or end of each day:

- Identify three things you are grateful for (e.g., people, experiences, small moments, or something in nature that brought you joy or a sense of peace).
- Write them in a daily gratitude journal.
- Pause and reflect on your list to fully acknowledge the feeling of gratitude.

You may also choose to share gratitude with someone directly via a note or text (a micro joy!).

REFLECTION

- How has expressing gratitude influenced your mood and well-being today?

Healing Together

Many Western self-care frameworks suggest that well-being exists in isolation from others. However, across African and diasporic traditions, well-being and restoration are sustained through community, relationships, and collective care. Others can help us process difficult experiences, share our joy, and remind us that we are not meant to carry life's burdens alone. The practices in this section highlight simple ways to nurture healing in community and to reconnect with the power of the village (see Chapter 5).

The philosophy of Ubuntu, present in many African traditions, deepens this understanding by emphasizing our fundamental interconnectedness. Often translated as "I am because we are," Ubuntu reflects the belief that our humanity is shaped and sustained through one another.

When we are experiencing Black fatigue, isolation can make the weight feel even heavier. Reconnecting with members of our village—friends, family, elders, and community—can help restore strength, connection, and hope. The practices that follow invite us to engage in healing together through storytelling, listening, and collective care.

REFLECTION BEFORE PRACTICE

- Who in your life feels like part of your village? What makes those relationships meaningful to you?
- When was a time you felt supported, seen, or held by your community? What made that moment significant?
- What kinds of support do you most need right now—listening, encouragement, practical help, or simply presence?
- How might healing Black fatigue in community feel different from trying to carry everything on your own?

Story Circles: Healing Through Storytelling

PURPOSE: TO CREATE SPACE FOR SHARED STORYTELLING, LISTENING, AND COLLECTIVE UNDERSTANDING

Storytelling has long been a foundation of African and diasporic cultures, as we have mentioned throughout this book.[8] Stories carry memory, wisdom, humor, grief, and survival across generations. When shared in community, storytelling can also become a powerful form of healing. Story circles create space for people to witness one another's experiences, affirm shared humanity, and remember that the weight of Black fatigue is not meant to be carried alone. In many communities, storytelling also keeps ancestral wisdom alive, allowing the voices and experiences of those who came before us to continue guiding the present (see Chapter 7).

Story circles can also be a meaningful way to support children and younger generations, who are not immune to Black fatigue, by giving them space to ask questions, share their experiences, and hear stories that affirm their identity and resilience.

WHEN TO USE THIS PRACTICE

This practice may be helpful when individuals or communities need space to share experiences, process emotions, and feel heard without judgment or interruption. Story circles can be especially meaningful when people are navigating shared challenges, reflecting on collective experiences, or seeking a deeper understanding of one another's journeys. They can also help build trust and strengthen connection within a group.

HOW TO PRACTICE

Gather a small group of trusted people.

- Choose a guiding question or theme for the conversation. Here are some examples to get you started:
    - Share a moment when you experienced Black fatigue. What helped you move through it?
    - Share a time when someone in your village supported you during a difficult moment. What did that support look like?
    - Share a moment when you felt deeply seen, affirmed, or understood. Why did that moment matter?
    - Share a practice, habit, or source of strength that helps you navigate challenging environments.
    - Share a moment of joy, rest, or resistance that helped restore your spirit.

  - Share something you have learned from your elders or ancestors about resilience or survival.
  - If elders are present, invite them to share wisdom or lessons about how they have navigated difficult times and what practices helped them sustain strength and hope.
  - If children or young people are present, invite them to share observations, questions, or stories in ways that feel comfortable for them. Listening to younger voices can deepen understanding across generations.

- Invite people to share their stories or reflections.
- Listen without interruption or judgment.
- Emphasize witnessing and understanding rather than fixing or responding.

REFLECTION

- What shifted for you when you shared your story or listened to someone else's?

Collective Celebration: Nourishing Joy in Community

PURPOSE: TO RECONNECT WITH JOY, COMMUNITY, AND CULTURAL TRADITIONS THROUGH SHARED MOMENTS OF CELEBRATION

Gathering in celebration is a form of healing. Music, laughter, movement, and shared meals have long created spaces where people reconnect with one another and with cultural traditions that sustain life. Food, in particular, often carries ancestral knowledge, such as recipes, ingredients, and practices passed down through generations that remind us of where we come from. Celebrating together can restore energy, strengthen relationships, and reaffirm our shared humanity.

WHEN TO USE THIS PRACTICE

This practice may be helpful when individuals or communities need moments of joy, connection, and renewal. Celebratory gatherings can help interrupt cycles of stress and remind us that our lives hold more than struggle.

HOW TO PRACTICE

- Gather with friends, family, or members of your community.
- Share food, music, laughter, or movement.
- Consider preparing or sharing a dish connected to your cultural or family traditions.
- Celebrate milestones, small victories, or simply the joy of being together.

REFLECTION

- What did this moment of celebration remind you about what it means to belong and to live fully?

Summary

Healing from Black fatigue is not a single practice or moment of insight—it is an ongoing process of returning to ourselves again and again. The practices in this chapter offer small ways to care for the body, clarify the mind, nourish the spirit, and reconnect with community.

Some moments of restoration may come through breath, movement, or reflection. Others may come through laughter, storytelling, or simply being in the presence of those who remind us that we are not alone.

Each practice is an invitation to restore balance, reconnect with joy, honor our humanity, and remember that healing is both personal and collective, sustained through the relationships that support us and the enerations who walked before us, walk beside us, and will come after us.

NINE

BUILDING A HEALING ECOSYSTEM

Rarely, if ever, are any of us healed in isolation.

—bell hooks, feminist writer and cultural critic[1]

Healing Black fatigue cannot be sustained solely through individual effort. For generations, Black people have understood that our ability to endure, restore ourselves, and continue forward in the face of racial stress has depended on the networks of care that surround us. Even in the absence of formal support, Black communities have created their own structures of care, as discussed throughout this book.

We have explored various aspects of healing Black fatigue, considering identity and belonging, our connection to the village, the role of our ancestors, the importance of resistance, and practices that support our daily renewal. In this chapter, we bring these elements together to envision a healing ecosystem.

The term *ecosystem* comes from ecology and refers to a community of living things interacting with one another and with their nonliving environment, each with its own role to play.[2] All the elements are interconnected. A healing ecosystem for Black fatigue is an interconnected network of relationships, practices, cultural traditions, and sources of support that sustain our ability to heal over time from the impacts of racism on our mind, body, and spirit. In the same way that ecosystems in nature depend on many interdependent elements to survive and thrive, our well-being is supported by the way these elements work together.

This chapter invites you to reflect upon and visualize the components of your own healing ecosystem, recognizing what is already present and what may be missing or in need of strengthening.

Mapping Your Healing Ecosystem

To help you reflect more concretely on the elements that support your healing from Black fatigue, we will walk you through a practice of visualizing your healing ecosystem. This is not about creating something perfect, but about making visible the systems that already support you. Using a tree as a metaphor, you will map the interconnected components that nourish, support, and sustain your journey toward renewal, joy, and reclaiming your humanity. Each part of the tree—the roots, the trunk, the branches, and the leaves and flowers—represents a different source of grounding, care, and connection.

As you move through this exercise, begin to identify what is already present in your life and where there may be opportunities for growth or strengthening. A sample completed healing ecosystem tree and a blank version are provided to support you as you map your own.

Roots: Cultural and Spiritual Grounding

The roots of a tree anchor it firmly in the ground while drawing in the nutrients and water it needs to survive. They provide both stability and nourishment, sustaining the life of the tree.

In your healing ecosystem, the roots hold knowledge, traditions, and practices that existed long before the conditions that gave rise to Black fatigue. They represent your sources of cultural and spiritual grounding, those things that nourish you, ground you, and keep you rooted. These include your ancestors and the values that guide how you move through the world, such as Ma'at, as well as spiritual ways of knowing, such as Sakhu, which speak to alignment and connection (see Chapter 2).

This grounding may also be expressed through cultural traditions such as music, storytelling, diasporic rituals, and food that carry ancestral knowledge and nourishment.

These roots remind us that healing Black fatigue is not only about what we do in the present, but also about what we inherit and embody, and what we remain connected to across generations.

REFLECTION

- What values guide you?
- What cultural traditions or spiritual practices ground you?
- Which ancestors do you feel connected to, and how do you stay connected to them?
- Which ancestors do you want to build a deeper connection with?
- What helps you feel rooted when you are experiencing stress or fatigue?

Trunk: The Self (Mind, Body, Spirit)

The trunk of a tree serves as its central support, holding it upright and connecting all its parts. It carries nourishment from the roots to the branches and helps maintain the tree's stability and balance. Without a strong trunk, the tree cannot sustain the life flowing through it.

In your healing ecosystem, the trunk represents the self—mind, body, and spirit. The impacts of Black fatigue, your relationships, and your daily experiences all move through and are processed within the self. This includes not only how you care for yourself, but also your understanding of your identity and the beliefs you hold about yourself. In the same way that a tree relies on a strong trunk, our ability to sustain ourselves depends on how we care for and support our mind, body, and spirit.

When the self is depleted, it becomes more difficult to access the support around us or engage in the practices that restore us. When the self is supported, we are better able to remain grounded, connected, and responsive to the elements that sustain us. As explored in Chapter 8, practices such as rest, movement, reflection, and breathwork offer ways to tend to the self.

REFLECTION

- In what ways do you currently understand or describe yourself, and how does that shape how you move through the world?
- How are you currently tending to your mind, body, and spirit?
- Where do you feel most supported? Where do you feel depleted?
- How do your current environments and relationships impact your well-being?
- What does your body need more of right now? (See Chapter 8 for a body mapping practice.)

Branches

The branches of a tree extend outward from the trunk, forming an interconnected structure. They support the leaves and flowers, allowing the tree to grow and reach beyond itself. Strong branches help to distribute weight and provide balance, helping the tree withstand external pressures. In your healing ecosystem, branches represent the relationships and spaces that support you—your village, spaces of belonging, and those who offer guidance and care.

Pruning branches is sometimes necessary to support healthy growth. There may be relationships or spaces that no longer align with your needs or support your well-being. Tending your ecosystem may require setting boundaries, creating distance, or letting go in ways that allow you to preserve your energy and make way for healing.

THE VILLAGE

Your village includes all the people in your life who offer care, support, and connection: your family, chosen family, close friends, elders, and others you trust. As we explored in Chapter 4, the village is a critical source of relational support, reminding us that we are not meant to navigate life or the impacts of Black fatigue alone. The village is rooted in mutual care—the ways we show up for one another, both giving and receiving. Your village can hold you in times of stress, celebrate moments of joy with you, and offer perspective when things feel overwhelming.

For many of us, the village may already exist informally, but there may be a desire to deepen this support by creating a more intentional and structured space for connection and healing. One way to do this is by cultivating a micro-village—a small, trusted circle of care grounded in shared intention, consistency, and mutual support.

HEALING PRACTICE: CREATING YOUR OWN MICRO-VILLAGE HEALING CIRCLE

Here is how you might formalize your micro-village:

1. *Start with intention.* Why do you want to create this space? Some examples of what a micro-village may focus on include:
    a. Restoring joy
    b. Collective grieving and release
    c. Stress reduction
    d. Workplace support
    e. Parenting and caregiving
    f. Cultural reconnection
    g. Creative expression

    An example of a purpose statement might be: *This circle exists to restore balance, connection, and wholeness through shared presence, stories, and practices that honor our ancestors and ourselves.* Being clear about your intention from the start can help shape the experience.

2. *Invite a small group.* Micro-villages work best when they are small enough to build trust. Consider inviting three to six people you feel safe with or would like to build a deeper connection with. You may invite one or two people and ask them to invite one or two people. You want to prioritize alignment with one another over the number of people in the group. Not everyone in your life is meant to be in your healing circle.
3. *Establish shared agreements.* Discuss and agree on how you want to show up for one another. Your shared agreements may include:

    a. *Confidentiality:* What's shared here stays here.
    b. *Reciprocity:* Everyone gives and receives; no one is "the strong one" or "the helper" every time.
    c. *Truth-telling:* Speak honestly but with compassion.
    d. *Non-judgment:* No fixing, shaming, or correcting others' experiences.
    e. *Presence:* Listen more than you speak.
    f. *Pace:* We move at the speed of trust.
    g. *Rest:* If someone needs silence or space, that is allowed.

4. *Choose a rhythm.* Will you gather in person, virtually, or a combination of both? Will you meet weekly, biweekly, or monthly? How long will you meet for? The format does not have to be complicated; what matters most is consistency and sustainability.
5. *Keep it simple.* Your time together might include check-ins, reflections, shared practices, or open conversation. There is no single right structure, and the space may evolve over time as the group's needs change.
6. *Sustain the space.* Like any part of your healing ecosystem, your micro-village requires care and attention. Reassess periodically to determine what is working and what may need to shift.

You will know your circle has become a true village when people begin to show up for one another beyond the space, offering support, sharing joy, and building trust and collective wisdom.

REFLECTION

- Who are the people you consider part of your village?
- Who do you turn to for support, care, or understanding?
- With whom do you feel safe to be your full self?
- Are there relationships you would like to deepen or strengthen?
- How do you show up for others in your village?

COMMUNITY AND SPACES OF BELONGING

While the village reflects our closest relationships, we also need spaces beyond those relationships where we feel seen, affirmed, and connected. These broader spaces that create the conditions for growth, resilience, and belonging are branches of our tree as well. They may include faith communities, affinity groups, sororities and fraternities, cultural organizations, or other settings that affirm your identity. Although these environments may not involve the same level of intimacy as your village, they still play an important role in shaping how supported, valued, and connected you feel—which, as we have discussed throughout this book, can significantly impact how we experience and respond to Black fatigue.

Many in-person and digital communities that focus on the wellness of Black people have emerged over the years. For example, OMNoire curates retreats and travel experiences centered on connection, care, and well-being for Black women and women of color.[3] Online spaces such as the Association of Black Psychologists' Sawubona Healing Circles offer opportunities for collective reflection, connection, and healing.[4] Community-based organizations such as the Black Emotional and Mental Health Collective (BEAM) support mental health and well-being by providing training, resources, and spaces for collective healing, particularly for marginalized communities.[5] Mutual aid initiatives such as The Okra Project, which provides support for Black trans communities, and local efforts like Black Lives Matter New Hampshire create additional pathways for care, resource sharing, and support.[6] Movements such as The Nap Ministry and platforms like the Black Joy Project center rest and joy as essential to well-being.[7]

REFLECTION

- In what spaces do you experience a sense of belonging and affirmation?
- What spaces and communities support your well-being?
- What environments leave you feeling drained or disconnected?
- What kinds of spaces would you like to seek out or cultivate?

HEALING GUIDES AND SUPPORT

Branches also support growth by connecting the tree to additional sources of strength and stability. Some branches reach toward light to access the energy needed to grow, while others provide balance and reinforcement. In your healing ecosystem, branches also represent healing guides and support, including those who offer specialized care, wisdom, or guidance. These may include therapists, spiritual leaders, coaches, mentors, somatic practitioners, doulas, herbalists, and other practitioners—these individuals offer tools, perspective, and care that complement what you receive from your village and community.

As we discuss in *Black Fatigue*, for many Black people, there is a stigma around seeking certain forms of support—particularly therapy. This stigma is shaped by historical mistrust, limited access, and cultural norms around strength and self-reliance. Choosing to seek support, however, is not a sign of weakness; it is a way of caring for yourself and expanding your capacity to heal, while also strengthening the ecosystem that sustains you.

There are spaces intentionally created by and for Black people that offer culturally grounded care, such as Therapy for Black Girls and

Black Men Heal, which provide access to Black therapists.[8] Organizations such as the Loveland Foundation and Therapy Fund Foundation support mental health through community-based approaches and financial assistance for care.[9] Practitioners such as Karen M. Rose, a Guyana-born herbalist and founder of Sacred Vibes Apothecary, carry forward traditions of plant-based and ancestral healing that connect wellness to culture and lineage.[10] Directories such as the National Black Doulas Association also help connect Black people to culturally aligned support and care.[11]

REFLECTION

- Who do you turn to for guidance, support, or specialized care?
- Are there forms of support you have been considering but have not yet explored?
- What kind of guidance would feel helpful to you right now?
- What would it feel like to receive support that is aligned with your values and lived experiences?

Leaves and Flowers: The Practices That Sustain You

The leaves and flowers of your healing ecosystem represent the practices that sustain and renew you. These are the daily, ongoing ways you care for yourself through rest, movement, reflection, breath, and moments of joy, as outlined in Chapter 8.

In a tree, leaves play a vital role in sustaining life. They absorb sunlight and convert it into energy, helping the tree grow and maintain its balance. Flowers, too, are a sign of renewal and reflect the tree's ability to thrive in the right conditions. In much the same way, the practices you engage in help restore your energy, support your well-being, and create conditions for flourishing.

As you consider this part of your ecosystem, think about the rituals, routines, and forms of care that help you feel restored, grounded, and energized. These might include the practices we explored in Chapter 8 and elsewhere in the book, or others you have discovered over time. As you incorporate them into your daily routine, you begin to create your own personal healing rhythm. For example, this might look like a grounding exercise in the morning, a moment of reset during the day, and an evening reflection with journaling, or a dedicated time to rest. It's important to create a rhythm that feels maintainable and supportive. The consistency of small, intentional actions makes the greatest difference in sustaining your ability to heal Black fatigue.

Just as leaves on a tree change with the seasons, some practices may no longer serve you in the same way over time. Letting go of what is no longer supporting you is not a failure—it is part of how your healing ecosystem adapts.

REFLECTION

- What practices help restore your energy and support your well-being?
- When do you feel most renewed or at ease?
- What brings you moments of joy, even in the midst of stress?
- What practices would you like to deepen or make more consistent?

Your Healing Ecosystem Tree

Now that you've reflected on the different elements of your healing ecosystem, it's time to begin mapping your tree. Figure 1 offers an example of how a healing ecosystem tree might look filled in with the elements outlined in the previous sections. We invite you to use Figure 2, a blank version of the tree, to write in the elements that most accurately reflect your current experience. There is no right or wrong way to map your ecosystem; there is only what is true and most meaningful to you.

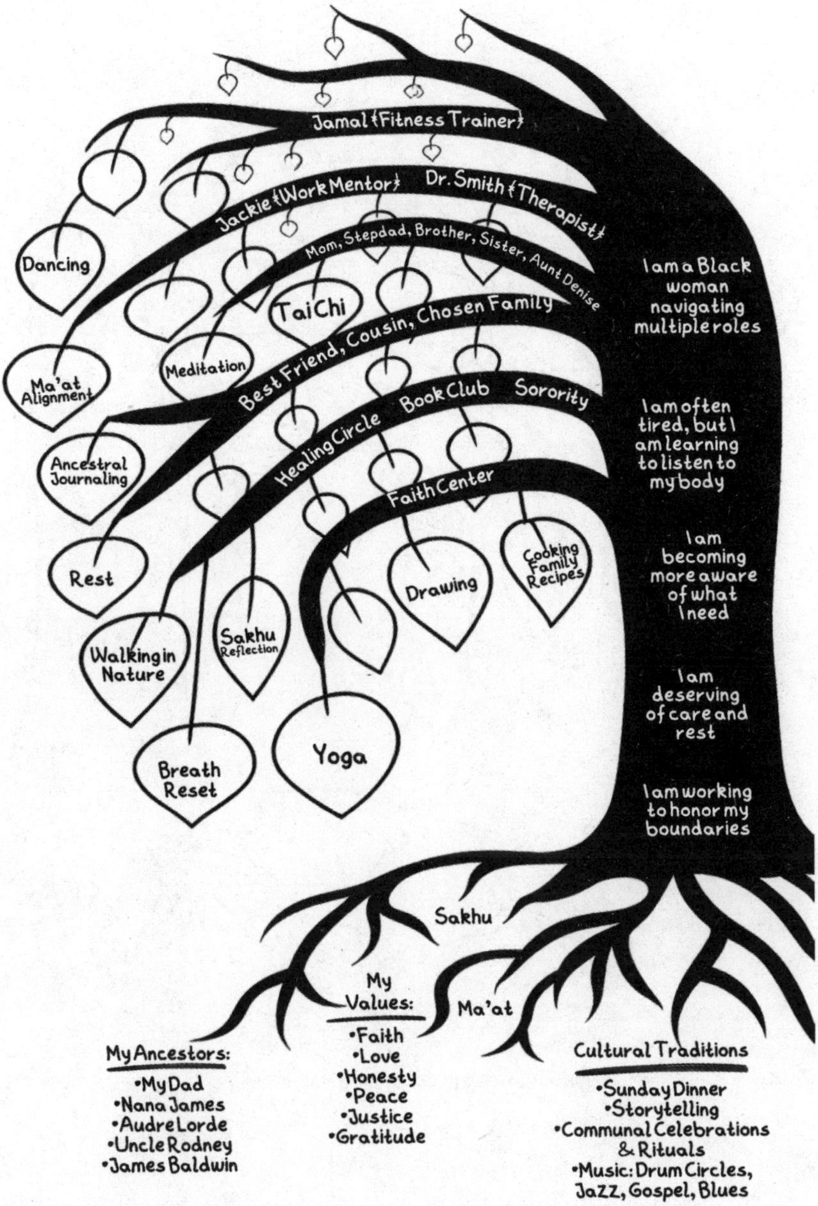

Figure 1. Healing ecosystem tree example

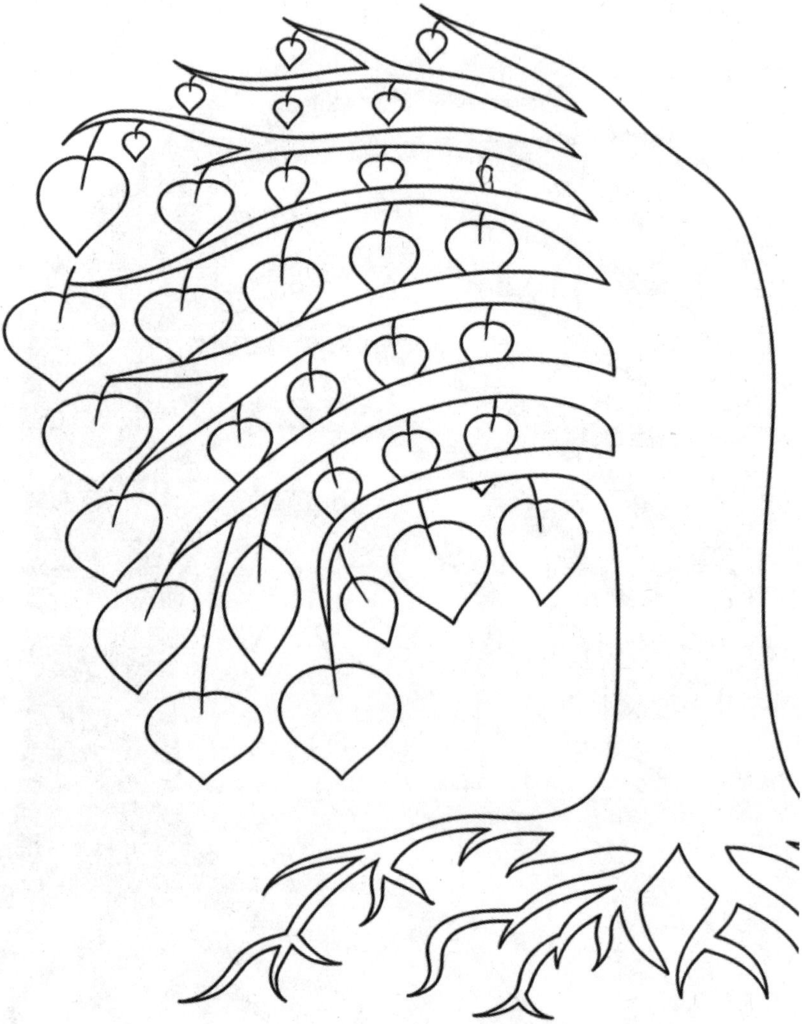

Figure 2. Healing ecosystem tree template

Use the reflection prompts in this chapter to guide you in completing your tree, placing your sources of grounding at the roots, your sense of self in the trunk, your relationships and spaces of support along the branches, and your daily practices in the leaves.

Some areas of your tree may feel full and well-developed, while others may feel sparse or still be emerging. We encourage you to be as specific as possible in what you include (e.g., using names of people or specific traditions rather than general terms). As you map your ecosystem, notice where you feel most supported and where there may be opportunities to deepen or strengthen your connections and support systems. We invite you to revisit, update, or recreate your healing ecosystem tree as your life shifts and your needs evolve.

REFLECTION

- As you look at your healing ecosystem map, what stands out to you?
- Where do you feel most supported?
- Where do you notice gaps or areas that feel underdeveloped?
- Which parts of your ecosystem feel most sustaining right now?
- What is one area you would like to strengthen or nurture moving forward? What support might you need to do so?

Summary

As you map your healing ecosystem and begin to see more clearly what supports you, what sustains you, and where you may need deeper connection or care, you become more intentional about how you move through the world and how you respond to the ongoing impacts of Black fatigue. Healing Black fatigue is not done in a day, or in isolation. It is something we must tend to over time and in community with one another. When these elements—our values, practices, relationships, and the spaces we choose to be part of—are aligned, they create the conditions for healing that is not only possible but sustainable.

Part IV

BUILDING A SUSTAINABLE FUTURE

Without new visions we don't know what to build, only what to knock down.

—Robin D. G. Kelley, historian, writer, and professor[1]

Living my ancestors' wildest dreams
I am the Global Majority
thriving & unbothered
I belong because I am
I am because we are

TEN

THE POWER OF THE GLOBAL MAJORITY

We know ourselves as part and as crowd, in an unknown that does not terrify. We cry our cry of poetry. Our boats are open, and we sail them for everyone.

—Édouard Glissant, French writer, poet, philosopher, and literary critic[2]

On the morning we started to craft this chapter, I (Mary-Frances) sat down at my computer to check my email and saw a comment on my LinkedIn page responding to something I'd posted nine months earlier about the co-opting of the term Black fatigue. At that time, there had been a flurry of social media posts about some white people declaring that they had "Black fatigue" because they were tired of Black people "misbehaving." This is my post that the commenter responded to:

I coined the term "Black fatigue" to name the emotional, physical, and generational toll that racism takes on Black people.

It's not about being tired of Black people, it's about the exhaustion of being Black in systems that were never built for us.

My book, Black Fatigue: How Racism Erodes the Mind, Body, and Spirit, *is grounded in research and lived experience. It speaks to*

> *the burden of microaggressions, the constant pressure to prove ourselves, and the very real health impacts of racism over time.*
>
> *Recently, the term has been misappropriated—most notably by a white TikToker in a now-deleted viral video ranting that white people are "tired" of Black people's so-called "ghetto, ratchet behavior," victimhood, loudness, and "blaming slavery" for today's inequities.*
>
> *Let me be clear, that is not Black fatigue. This term is not up for reinterpretation. It was created to affirm, not erase, the lived experiences of Black people.*

The new comment on this post is basically what this chapter is about. The commenter replied:

> *Seriously Black Fatigue should be a rallying cry for re-doubling our efforts to #doforself. . . . Black Fatigue will automatically be eradicated or significantly lessened the more we spend and keep the wealth re-circulating throughout the #BlackCommunity. We collectively need our own eBay, YouTube, LinkedIn, SoundCloud, cloud storage, etc that we can gate-keep since there are literally millions or hundreds of MILLIONs of #BlackProfessionals on this planet.*

They're right. There are 1.6 billion people living on the African continent, with an estimated 350 million more people of African descent living across the diaspora, including significant populations in Brazil, the United States, and the Caribbean.[3] People racialized as minorities who identify as other than "white" are actually the Global Majority, a term coined in the early 2000s by Rosemary Campbell-Stephens.[4] In fact, people of African (19 percent), Asian (58 percent), Indigenous, Latin American and Caribbean (8 percent), and mixed-heritage backgrounds constitute approximately 85 percent of the global population.[5] The global white population accounts for just 15 percent. It is estimated that by 2050, 25 percent of the world's population will be African.[6] But as we know, for the most part, the power rests in the hands of the numerical minority.

This chapter is important to healing Black fatigue because the idea of the Global Majority is not just demographic. It is a political, economic, and psychological reframing of power. It allows us to lift ourselves from under the white gaze toward transnational solidarity. It is a source of pride to remind ourselves that we are not the minority, taking us from a deficit lens to one of abundance. It helps us envision what could be possible if we collaborated, built self-sustaining systems, and reduced our dependency on the 15 percent who have historically extracted from, controlled, and oppressed us, with the reprehensible effects of that domination still present today. We imagine a world where equity, shared power, and a reclamation of our humanity are the order of the day in Chapter 11.

To answer the question of what is possible, we first need to understand a bit of the history that created these dependencies and the modern momentum to undo them.

Colonialism: A Global System of Domination

Colonialism was a systematic, global effort through which European powers expanded into Asia, Africa, the Americas, and Oceania from the 15th century onward. It involved conquest, resource extraction, cultural suppression, racism, and political domination.

The "Scramble for Africa," begun in the late 19th century, was one of the most aggressive examples of forced colonization.[7] Colonial powers from Britain, France, Germany, Portugal, Spain, Belgium, and Italy imposed artificial borders, extracted raw materials, and built infrastructure primarily to export wealth out of the continent. The ongoing economic dependency and political instability in many African nations trace directly back to this colonial pilfering.

European empires—particularly the British, French, and Dutch—also imposed economic and political control across South, Southeast, and East Asia. Colonialism disregarded established urban and cultural systems, replacing them with European-designed administrative centers and racial hierarchies. By the late 19th and early 20th centuries, major powers including Britain, France, Germany, Portugal, Russia, and Japan each controlled parts of China through economic, military, and political pressure.[8] China was partitioned into competing foreign spheres of influence that shaped trade and legal authority. These powers claimed territory, exclusive trade rights, and legal privileges, effectively sidelining Chinese authority. The effects of this disruption continue to shape patterns of urban inequality, governance challenges, and labor markets in many Asian cities today.

In India, British colonial rule imposed racialized social classifications such as "martial," "agricultural," and "criminal" castes—not to reflect Indigenous realities, but to divide populations, justify unequal treatment, and consolidate colonial control.[9] These externally imposed hierarchies hardened caste identities and left legacies that independent India later sought to redress through constitutional categories such as Scheduled Castes and Scheduled Tribes. Economically, colonial rule resulted in a systematic drain of wealth, the deindustrialization of traditional industries, and land revenue systems that triggered repeated famines while benefiting Britain's economy.

In the Caribbean, colonization involved plantation economies built on enslaved African labor and economic exploitation. The legacy includes unequal development, economic fragility, and governance structures still tied to European models.[10]

This brief overview provides historical context for understanding why many within the Global Majority continue to face systemic disadvantages in global trade, development, financing, access to technology, and geopolitical power.

The Rising Agency of the Global Majority Today

Despite the enduring impacts of colonialism and contemporary neocolonialism, we are witnessing the rising power of the Global Majority in a number of ways. As mentioned in Chapter 1, in March 2026, the UN passed a resolution declaring the trafficking of enslaved Africans the gravest crime against humanity. The resolution was presented by the president of Ghana on behalf of the fifty-four-member African Group, the largest regional bloc at the UN.[11] Other examples include collaborative efforts referred to as South-South partnerships, in which the 85 percent—who have historically been colonized, marginalized, and dehumanized—exchange knowledge, technology, and solidarity in ways that honor shared histories and collective struggle. These partnerships are not without challenges, but they reflect growing momentum toward greater agency, self-sufficiency, and reduced dependence on the 15 percent.

Here are some real examples of how South-South cooperation is reshaping development and expanding agency across the Global South:

- The UN Office for South-South Cooperation has created platforms such as South-South Galaxy, enabling countries from Africa, Asia, Latin America, and the Caribbean to share innovations, policy tools, and development models.[12] The *2025 Global Report on South-South and Triangular Cooperation* highlights how these exchanges are becoming increasingly central to global development.
- Brazil has emerged as a leader in people-centered development partnerships, offering expertise in hunger reduction and school nutrition to nations across Africa and Latin America.[13] In addition, since 2005 it has invested more than US$44 million in supporting other Global South nations through its partnership with the International Labour Organization.[14]
- Through growing interregional partnerships, policymakers from Asia-Pacific and Latin America are exchanging strategies on transitioning small and medium-sized enterprises (SMEs) to greener, more sustainable models.[15]
- Under the UN Development Programme's Climate Promise 2025, more than sixty countries across Africa, Latin America, and Asia are working together to strengthen national climate commitments.[16] These partnerships emphasize peer learning and development aligned with national priorities, not external prescriptions.
- Across the African continent, leaders are partnering with Latin American nations to share agricultural policies, strategies, and sustainable farming models.[17] These collaborations emphasize local adaptation rather than imported blueprints—a critical shift after decades of failed top-down development interventions.

While these examples offer hope for equalizing power and restoring agency to countries that have suffered from the lingering effects of colonialism, we must also confront a newer form of domination known as neocolonialism—modern systems through which powerful nations or corporations exert influence or control over less powerful countries. It's similar to colonialism without the old-style colonies. Examples of neocolonialism include high-interest loans that leave poorer nations burdened by debt, multinational corporations extracting natural resources with minimal benefit to local populations, and powerful countries influencing political outcomes in smaller nations.

One prominent example is China's expanding role in the Caribbean and Africa. China frames its development engagement as a "win-win" partnership rooted in Global South solidarity, positioning itself as an ally to nations historically marginalized by Western powers. Yet experts caution that behind this narrative lie significant power asymmetries that shape everything from financing arrangements to political leverage.[18]

In the Caribbean, analysts warn that large Chinese infrastructure loans can deepen dependency, raise concerns about sovereignty, and tilt negotiations in China's favor. Similar critiques have emerged across Africa, where China's Global South strategy is increasingly constrained by imbalanced trade relationships, reduced investment capacity, and strategic motives that do not always align with the long-term needs of African nations.[19] Understanding these dynamics is essential if the Global Majority is to build relationships rooted in genuine reciprocity, shared power, and collective liberation.

Yet despite the pitfalls, these initiatives show that we, the 85 percent, are no longer passive participants in a world shaped by others. We are designing, innovating, negotiating, and leading. Whether it's Brazil supporting African food systems, Asia and Latin America coinventing climate solutions, or Caribbean nations shaping their own development pathways, these collaborations demonstrate the power of the Global Majority to imagine new futures more grounded in mutuality.

The struggle for true equality continues, however, and we must be mindful and vigilant that neocolonialism can easily replace older forms of domination masking as equal partnerships.

How Can We Embrace and Uphold the Idea of the Global Majority?

Although efforts to harness the power of the Global Majority face significant challenges, the potential remains deeply hopeful for all of humanity. The legacies of colonialism continue to keep many nations in positions of disadvantage, while the rise of neocolonialism brings its own risks. But despite these realities, the growing influence, solidarity, and agency of the Global Majority offer possibilities for a more equitable future. Embracing the potential and promise of the Global Majority can also help heal Black fatigue. First, it requires a shift in mindset. We must reject language that minoritizes us, making us feel less than. Our extended selves belong to a "family" that spans across oceans; locating ourselves within this vast, living lineage reduces isolation and expands the resources available to us. Second, we must immerse ourselves in the history that brought us—the 85 percent—to where we are today. With that knowledge, we can hold our heads high, walk with pride, and reject false narratives with confidence and authority. Collectively, we hold the truth about who we were, who we are, and who we can become. Advancing the Global Majority advances all of humankind. The more progress we make on social, economic, political, and environmental issues that affect the Global Majority, the more the entire planet benefits.

As a member of the Global Majority, what can you do to heal the Black fatigue you might be experiencing by continuing to advance the power we have to effect change that uplifts us all? Here are some initiatives and actions to consider.

Sister-Community Partnerships

You might pair a US neighborhood group with a community organization based in Africa or elsewhere in the diaspora to exchange ideas and practices. For example, programs such as Partners of the Americas facilitate direct collaborations between US-based groups and Caribbean or South American organizations, allowing participants to exchange educational practices, cultural knowledge, and community-building strategies.[20] Similarly, initiatives such as Caribbean with Purpose connect US neighborhood groups with Caribbean schools and local associations to cocreate literacy and STEAM (STEM plus arts) projects, demonstrating how people-to-people connections can strengthen communities across borders.[21]

People-to-People Delegations

You can curate or participate in intentional trips that combine roots travel with skills exchange. For example, many organizations now plan small group journeys to Ghana that combine visits to historical sites such as Cape Coast and Elmina Castles with diaspora-to-local exchanges focused on cooperative economics, mental health practices, youth media training, and women-led entrepreneurship. Several Black women–led travel groups also arrange intentional trips to countries such as Ghana, South Africa, Senegal, Costa Rica, Jamaica, and Brazil, with explicit goals of Global Majority connection, cultural reclamation, and mutual learning.

Diasporic Funding Circles

Cross-border giving circles fund micro-projects ($500–$5,000) in both locales, emphasizing reciprocity, not charity. Small delegations travel to African and Caribbean communities to codesign credit unions, savings circles, agricultural cooperatives, or youth co-ops. As an example, Entrepreneurs Across Borders was created to connect experienced entrepreneurs, investors, and business leaders with emerging founders in developing nations.[22] The goal is to build bridges across borders.

Global Majority Value Chains

Throughout the Global Majority, we are witnessing the emergence of vibrant value chains—cultural, agricultural, technological, and educational ecosystems that circulate knowledge, resources, and creativity across borders. These value chains not only strengthen economic sovereignty but also deepen cultural connection and collective healing.

In the realm of culture, transnational collaborations are flourishing. Musicians across Africa and the diaspora are cocreating new sounds that blend ancestral rhythms with contemporary genres, including Afrobeats, while filmmakers such as César Díaz and participants in the

EU-LAC Próximamente Festival[23] are building cross-cultural film and arts collectives that link Europe, Latin America, and the Caribbean.

In food and herbal medicine, diaspora farm exchanges connect growers across continents who are reclaiming ancestral agricultural practices, preserving heritage crops, and stewarding land in ways that honor tradition and sustainability. Healing-herb cooperatives and women-led fair trade networks ensure that community wisdom around medicine, cultivation, and ceremony flows back and forth between villages, islands, and urban enclaves. These relationships not only support livelihoods but also nourish the collective body of our people.

The tech value chain is equally powerful. Young people across the Global Majority are building digital platforms that support community decision making and healing with tools for participatory budgeting, scheduling intergenerational healing circles, mapping local marketplaces, or capturing and archiving community stories. These youth-driven innovations demonstrate that technology can be rooted in cultural values and designed for collective well-being rather than extraction.

In education, open-access syllabi on diaspora history and African-centered studies, such as the freely available "Introduction to the African Diaspora" on OER Commons and MIT's Africana Studies courses, are used globally by educators and learners alike.[24] Likewise, multilingual resources such as open Creole and Caribbean identity courses help communities maintain linguistic roots while connecting across borders. In some Caribbean countries (e.g., Dominica, Martinique, St. Lucia), Creole has transitioned from being banned on school playgrounds to being embraced as a crucial part of national identity and school curriculum.

Together, these interconnected value chains form a living infrastructure for empowerment across oceans.

Somatic Healing at Scale

Some immersive trips—especially those led by Black therapists, somatic practitioners, or spiritual teachers—combine ancestral reconnection with collective nervous system practices, shared rituals, community rest circles, and workshops with local healers.

Somatic abolitionist Resmaa Menakem reminds us that communities carry shared bodies.[25] His idea of collective nervous systems teaches that groups of people absorb and transmit fear, stress, resilience, and healing across generations. These patterns live not only in individual bodies but in the relational field between us, shaped by our histories, cultural memory, and the repeated pressures of oppression.

Understanding ourselves as part of a collective nervous system is powerful for the Global Majority. It means that when we gather, breathe together, remember together, and practice care across borders, we are not just healing as individuals—we are regulating an intricate network that spans an entire people, softening trauma that has accumulated over centuries and strengthening the embodied capacity for liberation, joy, and connection.

Turning Barriers into Bridges

Working across borders can bring logistical and power challenges. Global Majority partners can adopt simple yet effective practices that make collaboration more equitable and sustainable. Language and time zone differences can be softened through bilingual facilitation, rotating meeting times that share the burden of inconvenience, and summary reels with subtitles so no one is left behind. Power imbalances can be addressed by cochairing meetings, sharing budgets transparently, and giving communities the ability to exercise real veto power over decisions that affect them. And when visa or travel costs pose obstacles, teams can rely on virtual labs, regional gatherings, pooled travel funds, and staggered delegations to keep momentum alive. These approaches help ensure that the focus remains on connection rather than obstacles.

REFLECTION

- To what extent do you feel a part of the Global Majority?
- How might embracing your belonging within the 85 percent help heal your Black fatigue?
- What practices can you adopt to make a stronger connection?

Summary

The power of the Global Majority is more than a demographic fact; it is a testament to our resilience, brilliance, innovation, and collective possibility. Remembering that we are part of the 85 percent allows us to reclaim a sense of belonging that connects us across borders, languages, and histories shaped by oppression. We step into a lineage that has not only survived but thrived across oceans and generations. This recognition alone is healing. It counters the isolation and exhaustion of Black fatigue.

When we claim this truth and look at ourselves through a lens of abundance rather than scarcity or deficit, we open up infinite possibilities. We begin to develop systems rooted in reciprocity instead of extraction, connection instead of coercion, and solidarity instead of domination. The Global Majority is already building this world through culture, cooperation, and shared learning.

Our task is to vigilantly keep the momentum going as agents of global transformation, ensuring that progress is fair and equitable. It won't be easy. Old systems are entrenched, and newer ones that are emerging risk imposing new forms of domination. But when we work together for the mutual benefit of the planet, we do more than heal our own fatigue; we create the conditions for renewal, joy, and the reclamation of humanity for all.

ELEVEN

REIMAGINING THRIVING WHOLE COMMUNITIES

Without community there is no liberation.

—Audre Lorde, writer, poet, and civil rights activist[1]

Authors' Note: In African diasporic traditions, storytelling has been used as a way of remembering, teaching, and healing. Stories carry wisdom across generations and help us to make sense of what has been. They also allow us to imagine what is possible. For that reason, we chose to write this chapter as a reimagination story.

It is not meant to describe a perfect world, but to offer a vision of what could be when the conditions that have shaped Black fatigue no longer exist. It invites you to step into a different way of living—one grounded in community, care, dignity, and shared responsibility

As you read this story, we invite you not just to observe the story, but to feel it. Notice what resonates. Notice what feels familiar. Notice what feels different. Notice what feels possible.

"A Day in a Thriving Whole Community"

Once upon a time—though not so long ago that people have forgotten, and not so distant that it feels unfamiliar—there existed a way of living for Black people across the African diaspora that required carrying a particular kind of weight, one that was harmful to their minds, bodies, and spirits. It was not always visible, and those outside of the Black community did not always believe it when told.

It showed up in the tightening of the chest when a police car slowed nearby, in the chronic stress, exhaustion, and illness that could not always be explained, in the careful recalibration of tone before speaking in a meeting, in the mental gymnastics that preceded even the simplest interactions, in the quiet calculation of whether one's presence would be questioned, challenged, or misunderstood.

It was a time when the underlying message for navigating the world as a Black person was some version of be careful, be aware, be twice as good, and be mindful of how you are seen. It was a time when excellence, competence, and credentials did not guarantee ease or promotion, when rest had to be justified, and when joy, though abundant, coexisted with a constant need to guard and protect it.

It was a time when Black fatigue was prevalent. Then, there was a shift.

Children in this world now listen to stories of "before" with curiosity. All they have known is a way of living grounded in care, connection, and a shared responsibility for one another. They cannot fully comprehend how people lived any other way.

The Shift

The elders call it "The Rebalancing." It was a moment born not out of revolution or conquest, but of a gradual, collective clarity. Black people across the globe began to recognize that the story they had inherited—one that had been forced upon them, insisting that humanity must be divided into us and them, worthy and unworthy—was too small to hold the truth of who they had always been, who they were, and who they were becoming.

It began with remembering. Remembering ways of living that had long existed but had not always been able to be centered, ways of being rooted in relationship, mutual support, and collective well-being. And as this remembering became stronger and took hold, something began to shift, not only for Black people and the Global Majority, but for the world around them.

The guiding belief of this shift was simple and sacred: I am because we are.

Morning Tradition

The day begins without a sense of urgency. Before anything else, there is a moment of pause and gratitude. Through the open windows, the air moves, carrying the sound of birds chirping and leaves rustling in the wind. The rays of sunlight bring warmth and a steady energy that feels like being held by the ancestors.

Throughout the home, the morning continues at an unhurried pace. Smells from the kitchen waft through the air, as one of the elders—a woman with smooth, dark brown skin that glows in the morning light—stands near the stove, preparing food for whoever from the community needs or wants to eat. There is always enough, and all are welcome. On the wall above her head is an engraved wooden plaque that reads: *Ubuntu—I am because we are.*

Before anyone begins to eat, she turns her attention to a small table set off to the side, filled with photographs of those who came before, a candle, and a few objects kept over time. She speaks softly, acknowledging the ancestors, and pours a libation in their honor. As people begin to gather—family, extended family, and others from the community—they pause at the table to honor the ancestors, each in their own way.

You enter the kitchen, greet those who have already gathered, and pay your respects to the ancestors. You fix yourself a plate and sit down to eat, taking your time. This time spent with family and the community is an essential part of your day. Once finished, you head out the door to go to work. As you pass by the shrubs that line the pathway to your car, you let your hand run across them and whisper, "Good morning."

The Neighborhood

You get into your car and ease out onto the street. People walk on the sidewalk, greeting one another as they pass. You drive slowly, waving and smiling at friends and neighbors. No one seems rushed. Young children are headed to school; some adults are on their way to work, while others are taking their daily morning stroll.

You've heard stories of what life was like before this time—before the reparations—but it's hard to imagine things being any different: that people of all walks of life and cultures did not always live together in this way, with the same sense of safety, stability, belonging, and ability to fully participate in the world around them. You are grateful that the ancestors fought for this, so you could live it.

Some of the homes along the block are newly built, while others have been passed down through generations and restored. The difference now is that we no longer live with the constant threat of displacement. There is no longer any question of how long we'll be able to stay or whether someone will try to buy us out.

As you continue driving, you pass a row of Black-owned storefronts. A sign above one reads *Johnson Family Grocers—Est. 2032*. Next door, a larger sign stretches across the front of another space: *Community Cooperative Market*. You pull over briefly, stepping out to grab a bag from your back seat—fresh vegetables from your family's garden. Inside, you set it down with the other food that has been brought in that morning and stop to chat with a few people nearby. This is a space where people take what they need and leave food and other items for others, paying what they can or nothing at all.

Back in your car, you continue down the road and pass one of your favorite bookstores. You've been told stories of a not-so-distant past when books about Black people were banned. That is now unheard of.

You stop at the next light, roll down your window, and acknowledge the police officer at the corner. "You coming by later?" you ask. They reply, "You know I wouldn't miss it." There was a time when this kind of exchange would not have been so easy for your people—when it could have brought anxiety rather than ease. Now it's just another part of the day. Policing is no longer about surveilling people or questioning their presence, but about ensuring the community's safety. You move forward without hesitation.

The Workplace

Before you walk into your workplace, you briefly glance at the bracelet on your wrist, given to you by your grandmother and engraved with the words *I belong because I am*—a gentle reminder that you carry with you. As you enter the building, you pass a wall of framed photos of past and present leaders. The faces reflect the Global Majority, with equal representation across gender identities. Black and Brown leaders are not the exception; they are expected.

On the way to your office, you walk past a TV on the wall and stop for a moment. A live government session is taking place. The president, a Black woman, leads the discussion, sharing updates on education, housing, and resource distribution. The conversation turns to preparations for the Global Convening taking place in your city this year. This annual gathering includes leaders and representatives from around the world and reflects a balanced and equitable distribution of power, with the Global Majority properly represented. During the Convening, there will be discussions on how to strengthen relationships and share technological advances, as well as ceremonies to honor the contributions of all living generations and the ancestors.

The workplace culture is one of mutual respect. Work is viewed as one part of life, not the core of one's identity. It is the norm to take breaks for rest and renewal during the day. There are wellness rooms throughout the building that offer space for employees to engage in daily healing practices as needed. Care is understood as a shared responsibility, and accessible, high-quality childcare is available in the workplace as a basic human right, not a privilege. Work schedules are flexible and shaped around the needs of the people doing the work rather than the other way around. Remote and hybrid options are widely embraced.

Everyone's unique contributions are valued. Pay is equitable, and expectations are clear. Boundaries are respected. You move through your workday without needing to adjust how you speak, present yourself, or position your ideas to appease the people around you. Your voice is heard as it is, and your contributions stand as your own.

The Gathering

At the end of the day, you make your way back home. As you turn onto your street, you can already see people beginning to gather. The sound reaches you first.

On one corner, a small group has formed, hands moving in rhythm against the surface of African drums. The beat, steady and familiar, carries through the space, weaving in and out of conversation. A few people of various generations have already begun to move to the music, hips swaying and feet naturally matching the rhythm. Others join in, clapping and laughing as they fall into sync with one another. Their joy is palpable.

You park and step out of your car, the sound of laughter rising around you as children run around playing tag, their energy contagious. Elders sit nearby, watching and calling out to them from time to time, smiling as they keep an eye on everything. You feel a tap on your leg and look down to see your little cousin at your feet, their arms stretched out, asking to be picked up. You oblige and kiss them on the cheek, and they giggle.

Tables have been set up down the block and in people's yards, filled with dishes brought by the community, along with photos and various mementos in remembrance of the ancestors. People move back and forth between tables, adding what they've prepared, uncovering trays, calling others over to eat. You stop at one of the tables and ask, "Is that Grandpa Jesse's sweet potato cornbread?" Your aunt smiles and responds, "You know that's the only recipe I use!" She's not your aunt by blood, but you have always called her that.

You make your way through the crowd, greeting people as you pass. Near the edge of the gathering, you spot the officer you saw earlier. "You made it," you say. "I told you I would," they reply with a plate already in hand.

You continue on, stopping here and there for brief conversations and shared laughter. Off to the side, a group of young people are seated at the feet of a few elders. They lean in, listening intently and fully present. One of the elders gestures as they speak, the others nodding along, occasionally adding something of their own.

Nearby, another group of children are gathered in a loose circle, passing something carefully between them. You glance over and recognize it's the trophy your youngest child won at the Annual Youth Innovation Challenge. They are animatedly explaining their winning project—a new way to ethically exchange data without harming the environment—as the others lean in, wide-eyed and excited, asking questions and taking turns holding the trophy. As the competition winner, your child will be honored as a special guest at the Global Convening.

You pause for a moment, taking it all in. The rhythm of the drums. The movement of bodies in sync. The smells of the spices from the food. The sound of laughter layered across generations. The ease and joy of being among one another. You are renewed.

As the evening begins to wind down, people start to gather closer to where the elders are seated. This is a tradition at the end of these gatherings. Before anyone returns home, the elders always tell a version of the same story.

A Story Told by the Elders

"Once upon a time," an elder with a calm, steady presence begins, "though not so long ago that it has been forgotten, there was a way of living that required some people to carry more burden than others." The children listen, their eyes fixed on the storyteller, some leaning into one another. The older generations have heard this story more times than they can count, but it is always a good reminder of the gratitude we owe our ancestors for not giving up on the fight for our humanity.

"It was a time when the world was divided in ways that did not reflect the truth of who Black people are. Others were given more access, more safety, more voice than we were. Black people often had to work harder just to be seen, just to be heard, just to live. During this time, people forgot that no one thrives alone and that borders were imaginary. They forgot that love was real. They forgot how to be human."

The children would gasp at this part, as if hearing a frightening myth instead of the reality of what once was. "But that doesn't make sense," one child says. "Why would it be like that?"

"It didn't make sense," the elder replies. "And yet, for a long, long time, it was the way of life." They pause to let the words settle. "There were people who spoke up and challenged what had been normalized. These people were your ancestors and their allies. They remembered a different way of being and refused to let it go. They organized, they resisted, they cared for one another, even when the systems around them made it difficult."

The storyteller looks around the circle, meeting the eyes of each listener.

"Over time, things began to change. People were fed up with what humanity had become, and they chose something different. They chose to dismantle the old and build a new system, one that honored the full humanity of all people. One that acknowledged the Global Majority. They chose to share power, care for the land, and distribute resources equitably, to ensure that no one had to carry more than their share again."

A small voice asks from the front, "Is that when things became like this?"

The elder nods, smiling. "Yes. That was the beginning of the world you know now." The children look around wide-eyed, taking in what surrounds them—the music, the laughter, the people gathered close.

"Will it always be this way?" another asks.

The elder smiles, not rushing the answer. "It will," they say, "as long as you remember."

"Remember what?" another child asks.

The elder leans back slightly. "That we belong to one another . . . all living beings. No life thrives in isolation, and the way we live is something we choose every day. I am because we are."

The crowd repeats back, "I am because we are."

And in unison, they repeat, "I am because we are."

The circle remains quiet for a moment longer before the sounds of the evening begin to rise again—the soft conversation, the movement, and the last notes of music carrying through the air.

The Ever-Becoming Future

This world is not perfect—no world shaped by humans ever could be—but it is honest, compassionate, and grounded in a shared commitment to dignity.

In this world, people still make mistakes and conflicts still arise, but they are now seen as invitations to deepen understanding. Disagreements are opportunities to practice empathy.

Over time, humanity finally came to understand that thriving was not a zero-sum game. One community's flourishing enriches all others, just as one community's suffering impacts us all. When those most affected by injustice are supported and able to heal, everyone benefits.

As this world continues, generation after generation, people return to what their ancestors taught them. We are ever-becoming and ever-remembering, not perfect but always whole.

We are a thriving community. A world where the Global Majority leads not through power over, but through power with. We are rooted in the simple sacred truth: I am because we are. And together, we rise.

REFLECTION

As you've just experienced, storytelling can be more than imagination; it can be a form of healing. It allows us to envision what has not yet fully come to be, while reconnecting us with what is possible.

The story you just read is one vision. Yours may look completely different. Take a moment to reflect:

- What would a thriving, whole community look like for you?
    - What would feel different in your daily life?
    - What would no longer exist?
    - What would be restored or reclaimed?
    - What role would you play in helping to sustain it?
- What is your thriving whole community story? We invite you to write that story as a healing practice.

CONCLUSION

CLAIMING YOUR POWER TO HEAL FROM BLACK FATIGUE

In this journey, we have invited you to explore identity, remembering, power, and global possibility, all in service of healing Black fatigue. As we come to the close, we invite you to pause, take a deep cleansing breath, and honor yourself.

You have turned inward to reclaim your sense of self and outward to recognize your place as a member of the Global Majority.

You have explored the deep ancestral roots that anchor you, the power that already lives within you, and the communities—known and unknown—that have always surrounded you with strength, wisdom, and love.

This book has been an invitation to remember who you are, whose you are, and what you are capable of creating, to facilitate healing from a world that insists on minoritizing us and creating false hierarchies that label Black and Brown people as less than, despite our numbers and our significant contributions to the planet.

And now, as we conclude with renewed resolve to carry our truth, the invitation grows: *Who will you become from here, and who will we become together?*

As you turn toward the future, let us review the journey toward healing Black fatigue.

Part I: Reclaiming Your Identity—Returning to Yourself

We began with the most fundamental of questions: *Who am I?* In a world that constantly tries to tell you who you are—by race, by gender, by stereotype, by circumstance—reclaiming your identity is in itself an act of resistance. You learned to look beyond narrow, externally imposed labels and reconnect with the fullness of your humanity. You discovered the layered beauty of an identity shaped by a rich history and culture.

Through African-centered psychology and Indigenous wisdom traditions, you came to see that you are not a fragmented being but whole with mind, body, spirit, community, and purpose intertwined.

You learned that healing begins with remembering that your identity is not merely who you are as an individual but how you are connected to your community, your ancestors, and society as a whole. We explored the concept of the extended self, which holds that you are not an isolated being navigating the world alone; you are an extension of your family, your lineage, your people, and your histories. You are also part of the Global Majority—the 85 percent whose ancestors built civilizations, cultivated sciences, imagined cosmologies, and gave birth to the human story.

This first part was about grounding. It was about anchoring yourself in your truth so that when you step into your power, your voice, and your agency, you do so from a rooted place—a place that cannot be shaken by the cruelty and dehumanization so often directed toward people of African descent and other marginalized groups.

Part II: Reclaiming Power, Agency, and Voice—Rising Together

With your identity redefined, you were ready to step into the work of remembrance, reclamation, and resistance. You revisited the concept of the village as a living blueprint for collective power. The village was never simply a place; it was a system of care, accountability, safety, love, and shared responsibility. Reclaiming it means refusing to internalize the lie that we must navigate life alone. It means recognizing that we need each other—and that relying on others is a sign of strength, not weakness.

Resistance, too, was redefined. Resistance is not only protest; it is also healing. It is living in a way that defies erasure. It is resting in a world that demands your exhaustion. It is choosing joy as an act of defiance. It is telling your story in a society that prefers your silence. It is protecting your energy, your boundaries, your gifts. It is saying *no more* to narratives that were never meant to reflect your truth.

In the workplace, you learned strategies to navigate spaces that were not built with your thriving in mind. You explored how to protect your psychological safety, how to find allies, and how to reconnect with your agency even in environments where you may be underestimated, undervalued, and disrespected. But you also learned that the workplace is just one arena and not the measure of your worth. You are bigger than any institution, title, or evaluation.

This section was about reclaiming your rightful place in the world. It was about saying: *I belong here. My voice matters. My power is real. My possibilities are endless.*

Part III: Healing Practices for Daily Renewal—Caring for Your Whole Self

Having reclaimed your identity, power, agency, and voice, you turned inward again. Healing is not an event but a daily practice, a lifelong commitment to yourself. In calling on the ancestors, you were reminded that you carry their breath, their prayers, their unfinished dreams. You walk with their guidance, their mistakes, their triumphs, and their courage.

You learned healing practices that nourish the mind, soothe the body, and uplift the spirit. These practices help you regulate your nervous system, reconnect with your inner knowing, and restore yourself from the ongoing assaults of racism, systemic inequity, and daily ~~micro~~aggressions, reminding you that your body is not the enemy—it is the vessel of your liberation.

From there, you built your healing ecosystem—a network of people, practices, places, and principles that support your well-being. Your ecosystem is your protective circle. Within it, you hold boundaries, rituals, joy, rest, spiritual grounding, creativity, and community. You learned that healing is not a solo act; it is a collective one. That the health of the individual cannot be separated from the health of the community. That rest, joy, play, music, dance, and connection are not luxuries; they are prescriptions for your healing.

This part was about restoration. It was about filling your cup, not just so you can keep going, but so you can keep becoming.

Part IV: Building a Sustainable Future—Expanding Your Circle of Belonging

Finally, you lifted your gaze to the horizon—to the future that the Global Majority has the power to shape. You explored the concept of the Global Majority not as a statistic, but as a paradigm shift. When we step out of minority thinking and into Global Majority consciousness, our posture changes. Our possibilities become infinite. Isolation begins to dissolve. We understand that humanity, culture, innovation, and beauty have always emerged from the Global Majority, and that the systems that have oppressed us were never reflections of our worth or capability; they were manifestations of someone else's fear and hatred.

You saw how nations and Indigenous communities across Africa, Asia, the Caribbean, and Latin America are building reciprocal partnerships—exchanging knowledge, cocreating solutions, and imagining models of development while continuing to resist neocolonial patterns. You learned how culture, food, technology, education, and healing can form value chains that circulate wealth and wisdom across borders.

You envisioned what it looks like for whole communities to thrive, rooted in justice, sustainability, equity, and collective flourishing. Communities where cultural traditions are honored, children grow up proud of who they are, economies are people-centered, and healing is woven into the fabric of daily life.

This part was about possibility. It was about reimagining not only how we live, but how we live *together*.

Coming Home to Ourselves, Coming Home to Each Other

As you stand here, at the end of the book but the beginning of your next chapter, we hope you can feel the immensity of your journey.

We hope you feel the ancestors at your back, whispering, *Yes. Keep going.*

We hope you feel the communities around you, cheering, *We are with you.*

We hope you can look in the mirror and say, without hesitation, *I am worthy. I am powerful. I am whole. I belong because I am. I am part of something vast and beautiful. I am because we are.*

When we traverse our history, we see one where those in power have tried, over and over again, to minimize and dehumanize us. But their efforts have not succeeded. We carry knowledge that predates colonization, capitalism, and every system designed to diminish our brilliance. We are the descendants of survivors, dreamers, visionaries, and healers. We are the inheritors of cultures that have shaped humanity itself.

Today, the Global Majority is rising to take its rightful place in the world. We are at the forefront of building new systems of cooperation, fostering innovative initiatives rooted in shared power and collective well-being.

We hope this book will be a companion, a reminder, and a guide supporting a healing journey rooted in greater resolve, confidence, and assurance.

ACKNOWLEDGMENTS

First and foremost we want to thank you, the reader of *Healing Black Fatigue*. Whether you come to these pages seeking affirmation, understanding, or tools for healing, we are grateful you are here.

Thank you to our family and friends for your unconditional support and encouragement throughout this journey. Writing about Black fatigue and, now, about healing requires us to sit with truth, memory, and emotion in very real ways. We are grateful for the village that holds us, sustains us, and reminds us of what it means to be whole.

We extend our deep gratitude to the individuals whose stories and lived experiences continue to shape this work. Your honesty, vulnerability, and truth-telling have been, and remain, a powerful force in helping to name not only the realities of Black fatigue, but also the pathways toward healing.

To the readers of *Black Fatigue: How Racism Erodes the Mind, Body, and Spirit*, thank you. Your engagement, reflection, and willingness to carry these conversations into your communities has affirmed for us just how deeply this work resonates. It is because of you—your stories, your questions, and your calls for more—that we felt compelled to expand this work. You reminded us that naming the harm was only part of the journey. Healing is necessary. Healing is possible. And healing must be collective.

We are also grateful to the many facilitators, practitioners, scholars, and leaders who have continued to bring the message of *Black Fatigue* into classrooms, workplaces, and movements. Your commitment to deepening understanding and creating change has helped sustain the momentum of this work and opened space for new conversations.

NOTES

Introduction

1 David Lanham and Amu Liu, "Not Just a Typographical Change: Why Brookings Is Capitalizing Black," Brookings, September 23, 2019, https://www.brookings.edu/articles/brookingscapitalizesblack/.

Chapter One

1 James Baldwin, "A Letter to My Nephew," *The Progressive*, December 1, 1962, https://progressive.org/magazine/letter-nephew/.

2 Leah Butterfield, "Black American Women's Roots Travel," *Annals of Tourism Research Empirical Insights* 6, no. 1 (2025): 100173, https://www.sciencedirect.com/science/article/pii/S2666957925000084.

3 African Ancestry, "Our Story," accessed January 11, 2026, https://africanancestry.com/pages/our-story.

4 National Endowment for the Humanities, "The Transatlantic Slave Trade Database," accessed January 4, 2026, https://www.neh.gov/project/transatlantic-slave-trade-database.

5 General Assembly, "Negro Womens Children to Serve According to the Condition of the Mother (1662)," *Encyclopedia Virginia*, December 7, 2020, https://encyclopediavirginia.org/primary-documents/negro-womens-children-to-serve-according-to-the-condition-of-the-mother-1662/.

6 United Nations, "UN Resolution Urges Reparations for Slavery's 'Historical Wrongs'," *UN News*, March 25, 2026, https://news.un.org/en/story/2026/03/1167199.

7 William E. Cross Jr., "Nigrescence Theory: Historical and Explanatory Notes," *Journal of Vocational Behavior* 44, no. 2 (1994): 119–123, https://www.sciencedirect.com/science/article/pii/S0001879184710086.

8 George Ella Lyon, "Where I'm From," accessed January 19, 2026, https://www.georgeellalyon.com/where.html.

Chapter Two

1 Wade W. Nobles, "From Black Psychology to *Sakhu Djaer*: Implications for the Further Development of a Pan African Black Psychology," *Journal of Black Psychology* 41, no. 5 (2015): 399–414, https://doi.org/10.1177/0095798415598038, 411.

2 Catalina Nam, "What Assumptions Underpin the Western Psychology?," Vision Psychology Brisbane, accessed January 19, 2026, https://www.visionpsychology.com/what-assumptions-underpin-the-western-psychology.

3 Olufunke O. R. Awosogba et al., "Contributions of African-Centered (Africentric) Psychology: A Call for Inclusion in APA-Accredited Graduate Psychology

Program Curriculum," *American Psychologist* 78, no. 4 (2023): 457–468, https://doi.org/10.1037/amp0001164.

4 Joseph Henrich, Steven J. Heine, and Ara Norenzayan, "The Weirdest People in the World?," *Behavioral and Brain Sciences* 33, no. 2–3 (2010): 61–83, https://doi.org/10.1017/s0140525x0999152x.

5 BLAM UK, "Language, Power, and the Global Majority," August 29, 2025, https://blamuk.org/2025/08/29/language-power-and-the-global-majority/; United Nations, "World Population Prospects 2024," accessed March 17, 2026, https://population.un.org/wpp/.

6 Informed by foundational scholarship in African-centered and Western psychology, including William E. Cross Jr., "Nigrescence Theory: Historical and Explanatory Notes," *Journal of Vocational Behavior* 44, no. 2 (1994): 119–123, https://www.sciencedirect.com/science/article/pii/S0001879184710086; Shawn Gingwright, "The Future of Healing: Shifting from Trauma Informed Care to Healing Centered Engagement," *Medium*, May 31, 2018, https://ginwright.medium.com/the-future-of-healing-shifting-from-trauma-informed-care-to-healing-centered-engagement-634f557ce69c; Hazel R. Markus and Shinobu Kitayama, "Culture and the Self: Implications for Cognition, Emotion, and Motivation," *Psychological Review* 90, no. 2 (1991): 224–253; Resmaa Menakem, *My Grandmother's Hands: Racialized Trauma and the Pathway to Mending Our Hearts and Bodies* (Central Recovery Press, 2017); Linda James Myers, *Understanding an Afrocentric World View: Introduction to an Optimal Psychology* (Kendall Hunt Publishing, 1993); and Nobles, "From Black Psychology."

7 Nobles, "From Black Psychology."

8 Wade W. Nobles, "Sakhu Scholarship," accessed January 25, 2026, https://www.drwadenobles.com/sakhu-scholarship.

9 Nobles, "From Black Psychology."

10 Nobles, "From Black Psychology."

11 N. J. van Blerk, "The Emergence of Law in Ancient Egypt: The Role of *Maat*," *Fundamina* 24, no. 1 (2018): 69–88, https://doi.org/10.17159/2411-7870/2018/v24n1a4.

12 R. James Ferguson, "The Ancient Egyptian Concept of Maat: Reflections on Social Justice and Natural Order," *Centre for East-West Cultural & Economic Studies Research Paper Series*, no. 15 (Bond University, 2016), https://pure.bond.edu.au/ws/files/25238910/The_ancient_Egyptian_concept_of_Maat_Reflections_on_social_justice_and_natural_order.pdf.

Chapter Three

1 Lawrence Stone, *The Family, Sex and Marriage in England 1500–1800* (Harper & Row, 1977).

2 Robert N. Bellah et al., *Habits of the Heart, with a New Preface: Individualism and Commitment in American Life* (University of California Press, 2007).

3 Orlando Patterson, *Slavery and Social Death: A Comparative Study, with a New Preface* (Harvard University Press, 2018).

4 Carol B. Stack, *All Our Kin: Strategies for Survival in a Black Community* (Basic Books, 1983).

5 Haenim Lee, "Determinants of Living in a Three-Generation Household Among Adolescents of Ethnic Groups in the U.S.: Family Structure, Social–Economic Status, and Cultural Factors," *Sustainability* 15, no. 13 (2023): 10460, https://doi.org/10.3390/su151310460.
6 Stack, *All Our Kin*.
7 Roy F. Baumeister and Mark R. Leary, "The Need to Belong: Desire for Interpersonal Attachments as a Fundamental Human Motivation," *Psychological Bulletin*, 117, no. 3 (1995): 497–529, https://doi.org/10.1037/0033-2909.117.3.497.
8 Kate Reilly, "How LinkedIn's HR Chief Is Changing the Diversity Conversation with 'Belonging'," *LinkedIn Talent Blog*, January 19, 2017, https://www.linkedin.com/business/talent/blog/talent-acquisition/how-linkedins-hr-chief-is-changing-diversity-conversation-with-belonging.
9 C. Eric Lincoln and Lawrence H. Mamiya, *The Black Church in the African American Experience* (Duke University Press, 1990).

Chapter Four

1 Ralph Ellison, *Invisible Man* (Penguin, 2014), 142.
2 Gwendolyn Brooks, "Paul Robeson," in *The Essential Gwendolyn Brooks*, ed. Elizabeth Alexander (Library of America, 2005), 113.
3 Infosys, "Racial Equity and Inclusion," accessed February 10, 2026, https://www.infosys.com/about/diversity-inclusion/racial-equity-inclusion.html.
4 Hillary Rodham Clinton, *It Takes a Village: And Other Lessons Children Teach Us* (Simon & Schuster, 1996), and "It Takes a Village," speech at the Democratic National Convention, Chicago, IL, August 27, 1996, https://www.americanrhetoric.com/speeches/hillaryclintontakesavillage.htm.
5 Ashley McGirt-Adair, *The Cost of Healing in Silence: Navigating Racial Trauma and the Call for Culturally Responsive Care* (Jossey-Bass, 2026).
6 Cassandra Lee Tellier, "Yoruba Culture," EBSCO, accessed February 8, 2026, https://www.ebsco.com/research-starters/history/yoruba-culture.
7 Authority Magazine, "Healing a Broken Mental Health System: Ashley McGirt-Adair of Therapy Fund Foundation on 5 Things That Can Be Done to Fix Our Broken Mental Health System," *Medium*, January 16, 2026, https://medium.com/authority-magazine/healing-a-broken-mental-health-system-ashley-mcgirt-adair-of-therapy-fund-foundation-on-5-things-3caa5c49edb2.
8 Connected Nation, "Bridging the Digital Divide: How Digital Skills Training Supports Black Communities," February 7, 2025, https://connectednation.org/blog/bridging-the-digital-divide-how-digital-skills-training-supports-black-communities.
9 Comcast, "Comcast Partners with The Hidden Genius Project to Help Black Male Youth Acquire Digital Skills and Enter the Tech Sector," press release, February 27, 2023, https://corporate.comcast.com/press/releases/comcast-hidden-genius-project-black-male-youth-digital-skills-tech-sector.
10 Tisha Lewis Ellison, Marva J. Solomon, and Delicia Tiera Green, "Centering Black Girls and Families' Digital Engagement, Reading (Literacies), Writing, and Interpretation of Multimodal Texts," *The Reading Teacher* 78, no. 6 (2025): 464–473, https://doi.org/10.1002/trtr.70003.

Chapter Five

1 Toni Cade, ed., *The Black Woman: An Anthology* (New American Library, 1970), 109.
2 Rebecca M. Kulik et al., "Nzinga," *Encyclopaedia Britannica*, accessed February 25, 2026, https://www.britannica.com/biography/Nzinga.
3 Raquel West, "Yaa Asantewaa (mid-1800s–1921)," Black Past, February 8, 2019, https://blackpast.org/global-african-history/yaa-asantewaa-mid-1800s-1921/.
4 Slavery and Remembrance, "Maroon Communities in the Americas," accessed February 25, 2026, https://slaveryandremembrance.org/articles/article/?id=A0060.
5 Erin M. Fehskens, "Nanny of the Maroons," Enslaved.org, accessed March 15, 2026, https://enslaved.org/fullStory/16-23-126814/.
6 Black Youth Project, "'Laughing Barrels' and the Defiant Spirit of Black Laughter," January 10, 2020, https://blackyouthproject.com/article/laughing-barrels-and-the-defiant-spirit-of-black-laughter.
7 Kendall Dooley, "Black American Christians: Hush Harbors and Holy Resistance," *BLK South* (blog), November 28, 2023, https://www.blksouth.org/blog/black-american-christians-witness-during-slavery.
8 "Ring Shout," in *Encyclopedia of Black Studies*, ed. Molefi Kete Asante and Ama Mazama (SAGE Publications, Inc., 2005), https://doi.org/10.4135/9781412952538.n219.
9 W.E.B. Du Bois, *The Souls of Black Folk* (A. C. McClurg & Co., 1903).
10 Jacob Uitti, "Behind the Meaning of the Classic Gospel Song 'Wade in the Water'," *American Songwriter*, February 3, 2023, https://americansongwriter.com/behind-the-meaning-of-the-classic-gospel-song-wade-in-the-water/.
11 Lois E. Horton, "Mutual Assistance: Building Black Community Life in Freedom," *History Now: The Journal* 60 (2021), https://www.gilderlehrman.org/history-resources/essays/mutual-assistance-building-black-community-life-freedom.
12 Howard Johnson, "Friendly Societies in the Bahamas 1834–1910," *Slavery & Abolition* 12, no. 3 (1991): 183–199, https://www.tandfonline.com/doi/pdf/10.1080/01440399108575041.
13 Audre Lorde, *A Burst of Light: Essays* (Firebrand Books, 1988), 131.
14 The Nap Ministry, "About," accessed March 15, 2026, https://thenapministry.wordpress.com/about/.
15 Du Bois, *The Souls of Black Folk*, 18.

Chapter Six

1 Alice Walker, *Possessing the Secret of Joy* (BCA, 1992), 102.
2 Cedric J. Robinson, *Black Marxism: The Making of the Black Radical Tradition* (University of North Carolina Press, 1983).
3 Mary Ellen Curtin, "Convict-Lease System," *Encyclopedia of Alabama*, last updated August 18, 2025, https://encyclopediaofalabama.org/article/convict-lease-system/.
4 Abbianca Makoni, "Black and Latinx Employees Face Bias in Job Performance Feedback, Study Finds," POCIT, July 20, 2022, https://peopleofcolorintech.com/front/black-and-latinx-employees-face-bias-in-job-performance-feedback-study-finds/.

5 Costas Cavounidis, Kevin Lang, and Russel Weinstein, "The Boss Is Watching: How Monitoring Decisions Hurt Black Workers," *The Economic Journal* 134, no. 658 (2024): 485–514, https://academic.oup.com/ej/article/134/658/485/7284382.
6 Ruth Umoh, "Newly Hired Black Workers Face Greater Scrutiny from Their Bosses, Study Finds," *Fortune*, January 31, 2024, https://fortune.com/2024/01/31/black-workers-new-hires-scrutiny-fired-unemployment/.
7 Psychological Agency, "Psychological Agency," accessed March 12, 2026, https://www.psychologicalagency.com/more-about-psychological-agency.
8 Elana Dure, "Black Women Are the Fastest Growing Group of Entrepreneurs. But the Job Isn't Easy," JPMorgan Chase, October 12, 2021, https://www.jpmorgan.com/insights/business-planning/black-women-are-the-fastest-growing-group-of-entrepreneurs-but-the-job-isnt-easy.
9 Amanda Chua, "Bridging the Qualitative vs Quantitative Performance Measurement Gap," *Omni* (blog), November 20, 2025, https://www.omnihr.co/blog/qualitative-vs-quantitative-examples.
10 Janice Gasam Asare, *Rise and Resist: How to Reclaim Workplace Equity and Justice* (Berrett-Koehler Publishers, 2026), 65.

Chapter Seven

1 Resmaa Menakem, *The Quaking of America: An Embodied Guide to Navigating Our Nation's Upheaval and Racial Reckoning* (Central Recovery Press, 2022), 4.
2 Maya Angelou, "Our Grandmothers," in *I Shall Not Be Moved* (Random House, 1990).
3 See e.g. The Historic Present, "Alexander Hamilton Was Not Black," May 11, 2016, https://thehistoricpresent.com/2016/05/11/alexander-hamilton-was-not-black/.
4 Jane Bakewell, "BVI Wall Murals Are Open-Air Museums," *The BVI Insider*, accessed March 9, 2026, https://thebviinsider.com/bvi-wall-murals-open-air-museums/.
5 Resmaa Menakem, *My Grandmother's Hands: Racialized Trauma and the Pathway to Mending Our Hearts and Bodies* (Central Recovery Press, 2017).
6 Weekend Nation, "A First for Female Drummers," March 6, 2026.

Chapter Eight

1 Toni Morrison, *Song of Solomon* (Knopf, 1977), 337.
2 Resmaa Menakem, *My Grandmother's Hands: Racialized Trauma and the Pathway to Mending Our Hearts and Bodies* (Central Recovery Press, 2017).
3 Mayo Clinic, "Exercise and Stress: Get Moving to Manage Stress," September 19, 2025, https://www.mayoclinic.org/healthy-lifestyle/stress-management/in-depth/exercise-and-stress/art-20044469.
4 Glo Atanmo (@glographics), "Some comfort words from my latest podcast episode," Instagram photo, July 12, 2025, https://www.instagram.com/p/DMBmXLmslfH/.
5 The Nap Ministry, "About," accessed March 15, 2026, https://thenapministry.wordpress.com/about/.
6 Nina Green, "7 Ways Gratitude Rewires Your Brain: The Science Behind a Powerful Practice," *Center for NeuroWellness Blog*, September 27, 2024, https://centerforneurowellness.com/gratitude-brain/.

7 Maureen Salamon, "Gratitude Enhances Health, Brings Happiness—and May Even Lengthen Lives," *Harvard Health Blog*, September 11, 2024, https://www.health.harvard.edu/blog/gratitude-enhances-health-brings-happiness-and-may-even-lengthen-lives-202409113071.

8 See also Chioma Alaedu, "The Role of Storytelling and Oral Traditions in Preserving African Culture," *Primer Africa*, August 25, 2024, https://primerafrica.blog/the-role-of-storytelling-and-oral-traditions-in-preserving-african-culture/.

Chapter Nine

1 bell hooks, *All About Love: New Visions* (Perennial, 2001), 215.

2 Melissa Murray, "What Is an Ecosystem?," Australian Museum, last updated February 25, 2025, https://australian.museum/learn/species-identification/ask-an-expert/what-is-an-ecosystem/.

3 OMNoire, "Home," accessed March 30, 2026, https://omnoire.com.

4 The Association of Black Psychologists, Inc., "Sawubona Healing Circles," accessed March 30, 2026, https://abpsi.org/sawubona/.

5 Black Emotional and Mental Health Collective, "About Us," accessed March 30, 2026, https://beam.community.

6 The Okra Project, "About," accessed March 30, 2026, https://www.theokraproject.com; Black Lives Matter New Hampshire, "Mutual Aid Fund," accessed March 30, 2026, https://blmnh.org/mutual-aid-fund.

7 The Nap Ministry, "About," accessed March 15, 2026, https://thenapministry.wordpress.com/about/; Kleaver Cruz, "The Black Joy Project," accessed March 30, 2026, https://kleavercruz.com/the-black-joy-project/.

8 Therapy for Black Girls, "Our Mission," accessed March 25, 2026, https://therapyforblackgirls.com/about/; Black Men Heal, "About Us," accessed March 28, 2026, https://blackmenheal.org/all-about-us/.

9 The Loveland Foundation, "About Us," accessed March 25, 2026, https://thelovelandfoundation.org/about/; Therapy Fund Foundation, "About," accessed March 25, 2026, https://therapyfundfoundation.org/about.

10 Sacred Vibes Apothecary, "About," accessed March 25, 2026, https://www.sacredvibeshealing.com/about-sacred-vibes.

11 National Black Doulas Association, "Home," accessed March 25, 2026, https://www.blackdoulas.org.

Chapter Ten

1 Robin D. G. Kelley, *Freedom Dreams: The Black Radical Imagination* (Beacon Press, 2002), xii.

2 Édouard Glissant, "The Open Boat," in *The Poetics of Relation*, trans. Betsy Wing (University of Michigan Press, 1997), 9.

3 Worldometer, "Africa Population," accessed March 29, 2026, https://www.worldometers.info/world-population/africa-population/; State of the African Diaspora, "The African Diaspora," accessed March 29, 2026, https://thestateofafricandiaspora.com/the-african-diaspora/.

4 BLAM UK, "Language, Power, and the Global Majority," August 29, 2025, https://blamuk.org/2025/08/29/language-power-and-the-global-majority/.

5 United Nations, "World Population Prospects 2024," accessed March 17, 2026, https://population.un.org/wpp/.

6 Worldometer, "Africa Population."

7 *Britannica*, "Scramble for Africa," last updated January 17, 2026, https://www.britannica.com/event/Scramble-for-Africa.

8 *Britannica*, "Western Colonialism: The Open Door Policy," last updated February 9, 2026, https://www.britannica.com/topic/Western-colonialism/The-Open-Door-Policy.

9 Sociology Institute, "British Colonial Views on Indian Castes and Tribes: Implications for Sociology," last updated August 15, 2025, https://sociology.institute/sociology-in-india/british-colonial-views-indian-castes-tribes-sociology/.

10 Colin Clarke, "Establishment of the Colonial Empire: Sugar-Slave Plantations, White Exploitation, and Slave Suppression," in *Racist Regimes, Forced Labour and Death* (Palgrave Macmillan, 2024), 29–59.

11 UN News, "UN Resolution Urges Reparations for Slavery's 'Historical Wrongs'," March 25, 2026, https://news.un.org/en/story/2026/03/1167199.

12 South-South Galaxy, "About Us," accessed March 28, 2026, https://southsouth-galaxy.org/about/.

13 United Nations, "Partnerships in the Global South: How South-South Cooperation Is Driving Development," September 3, 2025, https://social.desa.un.org/world-summit-2025/blog/partnerships-in-the-global-south-how-south-south-cooperation-is-driving.

14 International Labour Organization, "United Nations Day for South-South Cooperation 2025," news release, September 12, 2025, https://www.ilo.org/resource/news/united-nations-day-south%E2%80%93south-cooperation-2025.

15 Economic and Social Commission for Asia and the Pacific, "Bridging Continents: Advancing Sustainable Development Through South-South Cooperation," news release, May 20, 2025, https://www.unescap.org/news/bridging-continents-advancing-sustainable-development-through-south-south-cooperation.

16 United Nations, "Partnerships in the Global South."

17 Krsna Powell, "When Cooperation Moves Beyond Capitals: Building South-South Partnerships That Deliver," *Africa Practice*, October 6, 2025, https://africapractice.com/insights/bridging-continents-building-futures-south-south-cooperation-for-africas-next-horizon/.

18 PolSci Institute, "Neo-Colonialism: Modern Exploitation of Developing Countries by the Developed World," last updated October 26, 2025, https://polsci.institute/international-relations/neo-colonialism-modern-exploitation-developing-countries/.

19 Naveen Sharma, "China in Africa: Soft Power and the Development of Neocolonial States," *Cornell Undergraduate Research Journal* 2, no. 1 (2023): 75–85, https://doi.org/10.37513/curj.v2i1.716.

20 Partners of the Americas, "The Power of People-to-People Exchange," accessed March 25, 2026, https://www.partners.net/our_stories/the-power-of-people-to-people-exchange/.

21 Caribbean with Purpose, "Community Organizations," accessed March 25, 2026, https://caribbeanwithpurpose.org/community-organizations/.

22 Entrepreneurs Across Borders, "Working to Create a Better Tomorrow for Emerging Economies," accessed March 28, 2026, https://www.eaborders.org/about/.
23 European Union External Action, "How Diaspora Artists Create Cultural Bridges Among Cultures and Societies," April 2, 2025, https://www.eeas.europa.eu/eeas/how-diaspora-artists-create-cultural-bridges-among-cultures-and-societies_en.
24 OER Commons, "HIST 350: Introduction to the African Diaspora Syllabus 2020," accessed March 28, 2026, https://oercommons.org/courseware/lesson/115935; MIT OpenCourseWare, "Africana Studies," accessed March 28, 2026, https://ocw.mit.edu/course-lists/africana-studies/.
25 Resmaa Menakem, *My Grandmother's Hands: Racialized Trauma and the Pathway to Mending Our Hearts and Bodies* (Central Recovery Press, 2017).

Chapter Eleven

1 Audre Lorde, "The Master's Tools Will Never Dismantle the Master's House," in *Sister Outsider: Essays and Speeches* (Crossing Press, 1984), 112.

INDEX

C

ABOUT THE AUTHORS

Mary-Frances Winters (she/her/hers) came of age during the civil rights movement of the 1960s. Starting with her days as editor of her high school newspaper, she realized that diversity, equity, inclusion, and justice work is her "passion and calling." Founding The Winters Group in 1984 was the next step in fulfilling what she believes is her true purpose on this earth—breaking down barriers and building bridges across differences. As CEO of The Winters Group, she has been able to magnify the impact of her thought-provoking message.

Mary-Frances is a master strategist with experience in strategic planning, change management, diversity, organization development, training and facilitation, systems thinking, and qualitative and quantitative research methods. She has extensive experience in working with senior leadership teams to drive organizational change.

Among her many awards and distinctions, Mary-Frances was named a diversity pioneer by *Profiles in Diversity Journal* in 2007 and received the journal's Black Leadership Award in 2023. In 2023, she was named to the Top 25 Restorative People Leaders Watchlist. She is also the 2016 recipient of the Winds of Change Award from the Forum on Workplace Inclusion. In addition, she was featured in the June 2016 publication of *Forbes*, which honored some of the DC Metro area's most powerful women. In November 2019, Mary-Frances was named by *Forbes* as one of ten trailblazers in diversity and inclusion. She was accepted into the Forbes Business Council in 2023.

Mary-Frances has served as a torchbearer for the Olympics and has been recognized as an Athena Award winner by the Greater Rochester Chamber of Commerce for her contributions to women and the community.

In addition to *Healing Black Fatigue*, Mary-Frances is the author of seven books: *Black Fatigue: How Racism Erodes the Mind, Body, and Spirit*; *We Can't Talk About That at Work!: How to Talk About Race, Religion, Politics, and Other Polarizing Topics*; *Racial Justice at Work: Practical Solutions for Systemic Change*; *Inclusive Conversations: Fostering Equity, Empathy, and Belonging Across Differences*; *Only Wet Babies Like Change: Workplace Wisdom for Baby Boomers*; *Inclusion Starts with "I"—Eight Steps to Inclusion: The Personal Journey*; and *CEOs Who Get It: Diversity Leadership from the Heart and Soul*. She has also authored a chapter in the book *Diversity at Work: The Practice of Inclusion* and numerous articles.

Mary-Frances is a graduate of the University of Rochester, with undergraduate degrees in English and psychology and a master's degree in business administration from the William E. Simon Executive Development Program. She was the first Black woman elected to the University of Rochester's Board of Trustees. She received an honorary doctorate from Roberts Wesleyan College.

Mareisha N. Winters Reese (she/her/hers) is a Xennial (cusp of Millennial and Generation X) Black woman who serves as president and chief operating officer at The Winters Group. In this role, Mareisha manages the day-to-day operations of the organization. She joined the company in 2012 as vice president to help develop new products, bring in new business, service clients, manage social media, and research and consult.

Prior to joining The Winters Group, Mareisha worked as a software engineer for a large defense contractor. The experience of often being the only Black woman in her workspaces, and the biases and microaggressions that came along with that, fueled her passion for diversity, equity, inclusion, and justice work. She took that passion to her role as program manager for HBCU-UP at Johnson C. Smith University, a National Science Foundation grant–funded program to recruit, retain, and graduate underrepresented students in STEM fields.

Mareisha earned a bachelor of science in computer science from Spelman College, a bachelor of science in electrical engineering from Georgia Tech, and dual master's degrees in business administration and information systems from the University of Maryland's Robert H. Smith School of Business. She is currently pursuing her PhD in organizational development and change at Fielding Graduate University.

In 2021, Mareisha was named one of Diversity MBA's Top 100 Under 50 Executive and Emerging Leaders and to Diversity Woman Media's The Power 100 List. In 2023, she was recognized with a Women Worth Watching in Leadership Award from *Profiles in Diversity Journal* and was named one of the *Charlotte Business Journal*'s Power 100 for

DEI. She was also included on the 2025 Top 25 Restorative People Leaders Watchlist.

Mareisha is coauthor of *Black Fatigue: How Racism Erodes the Mind, Body, and Spirit*; *We Can't Talk About That at Work!: How to Talk About Race, Religion, Politics, and Other Polarizing Topics*; and *Racial Justice at Work: Practical Solutions for Systemic Change.*

ABOUT THE WINTERS GROUP, INC.

The Winters Group, Inc., is a Black women–owned global organizational change and development consulting firm specializing in diversity, equity, inclusion, and justice (DEIJ). Since 1984, The Winters Group has been committed to unapologetically challenging systems of oppression and reimagining what it means to create cultures of true equity and inclusion. Grounded in lived experience, research-informed practice, and more than four decades of partnership with organizations across industries, The Winters Group empowers leaders to drive systemic change and cultivate human-centered workplaces where everyone can thrive.

Clients, ranging from Fortune 100 corporations to educational institutions, nonprofits, and global organizations, turn to The Winters Group for bold, transformational support. Our offerings include culture and equity audits and assessments, strategy development and implementation, customized learning experiences, executive coaching, and thought leadership that centers on the voices and experiences of those historically marginalized.

The Winters Group also advances social impact through Live Inclusively® Actualized, its philanthropic arm dedicated to dismantling systemic barriers through grantmaking, service, and community partnerships.

For more information, visit wintersgroup.com.

Also by Mary-Frances Winters and Mareisha N. Reese

Black Fatigue, Second Edition

How Racism Erodes the Mind, Body, and Spirit

The pioneering book that exposed the intergenerational health impacts of systemic racism is back to meet the demands of our post-2020 reality.

Black people are exhausted. The toll of living within systems designed to exclude them devastates minds, bodies, and spirits. With unflinching honesty and a practical lens, Winters and Reese document the enduring toll of "living while Black" while also equipping readers with strategies for personal healing and organizational transformation.

We Can't Talk about That at Work! Second Edition

How to Talk about Race, Religion, Politics, and Other Polarizing Topics

Politics, religion, race—we can't talk about topics like these at work, right? But in fact, these conversations are happening all the time. And if they aren't handled effectively, they can become more polarizing and divisive, impacting productivity, engagement, retention, teamwork, and even employees' sense of safety in the workplace.

Featuring a new chapter, as well as a discussion guide and updated glossary, this modern classic offers step-by-step guidance for conducting structured conversations around polarizing topics.

Also by Mary-Frances Winters

Inclusive Conversations

Fostering Equity, Empathy, and Belonging across Differences

In this book, Mary-Frances Winters offers specific dialogue strategies to foster greater understanding on the following topics:

- Recognizing the importance of creating equity and sharing power
- Dealing with the "fragility" of dominant groups--their discomfort in engaging with historically subordinated groups
- Addressing the exhaustion historically marginalized groups feel from constantly explaining their different lived experience
- Exploring how to build trust and create psychologically safe spaces for dialogue

Racial Justice at Work

Practical Solutions for Systemic Change

Traditional DEI work has not succeeded at dismantling systems that perpetuate harm and exclude BIPOC groups. Creating justice-centered organizations is the next frontier in DEI.

Mary-Frances Winters and her coauthors address some of the most significant aspects of adding a justice focus to diversity work, showing how to create a workplace culture where equity is not a checklist of performative actions but a lived reality.

Berrett-Koehler
PUBLISHERS

Dear Reader,

Welcome to the Berrett-Koehler Community—a global network of changemakers creating positive impact in their lives, organizations, and communities.

Our Mission: Connecting People and Ideas to Create a World That Works for All

We believe transformation is possible. While outdated paradigms of self-interest, exclusion, and hierarchy continue to hold back our communities and organizations, we know that change can happen. That's why we connect people with actionable ideas from leading experts who are already creating the solutions we need.

The BK Way

We're an independent publisher that practices what we publish. Our books, digital resources, and community offerings provide practical pathways for building more just, equitable, and sustainable organizations and lives. Whether you're transforming your workplace, community, or personal practices, our publications meet you where you are with tools that work.

But we don't just talk about positive change—we live it. Through "The BK Way," we put stewardship and purpose before profit. As a benefit corporation, we're legally committed to benefiting all our stakeholders: authors, readers, employees, communities, and the environment.

As our gift to you, claim your free bestselling ebook at bkconnection .com/welcome. You'll also receive fresh leadership insights delivered to your inbox from bkconnection.com/blogs/the-bk-exchange.

You Make the Difference

We're grateful to our readers, authors, and community members, who bring our mission to life every day. Your stories of transformation inspire us and show others what's possible.

Share how BK publications are making a difference in your world at bkconnection.com/impact.

Your friends at Berrett-Koehler

Join the Berrett-Koehler Community

Are you passionate about supporting independent publishing and reading diverse voices and perspectives? Join the BK Community Membership Program and become a part of a vibrant literary community. To support mission-based publishing while saving up to 30 percent on all books and attending exclusive events, visit ideas.bkconnection.com/bkcommunity-join to learn more and become a member.

MIX
Paper | Supporting responsible forestry
FSC® C005010
FSC
www.fsc.org